DONALD GRAVES IN AUSTRALIA—
"Children want to write . . ."

edited by R.D. Walshe
<small>PUBLICATIONS EDITOR, P.E.T.A.</small>

Primary English Teaching Association

Acknowledgments

PETA records its thanks to many people who have made this book possible:

- *For a generous grant to assist printing costs:* NSW State Development Committee (In-service Education)
- *For cover design:* Dorothy Dunphy
- *For layout and typesetting:* Les Speirs, and G & L Typesetters
- *For printing:* John Rough, and Bridge Printery Pty. Ltd.
- *For photographs:* Barbara Kamler, Riverina C.A.E. (pp. 73, 97); Sydney Morning Herald (cover); Writing Process Laboratory, the University of New Hampshire
- *For permission to reprint articles:*

Ch. 1: Donald H. Graves, and Organising Committee of Third International Conference on the Teaching of English.

Ch. 2: Susan Sowers.

Ch. 3: Susan Sowers, and 'Learning, the Magazine for Creative Teaching', California USA.

Ch. 4: Lucy McCormick Calkins, and the National Association of Elementary School Principals, Virginia USA, for this article, which appeared under the title 'Work in Progress: One School's Writing Program' in 'National Elementary Principal', Vol. 59, No. 4, June 1980: Copyright 1980, National Association of Elementary School Principals: All rights reserved.

Ch. 5: Donald H. Graves.

Ch. 6: Lucy McCormick Calkins, and 'Language Arts', February 1980, NCTE, Illinois USA.

Ch. 7: Barbara Kamler, and 'Language Arts', September 1980, NCTE, Illinois USA.

Ch. 8: Lucy McCormick Calkins, and 'Language Arts', May 1980, NCTE, Illinois USA.

Ch. 9: Judith E. Egan.

Ch. 10: Mary Ellen Giacobbe, and 'Learning, the Magazine for Creative Teaching', California USA.

Ch. 11: Donald H. Graves and Donald M. Murray, and the 'Journal of Education', Boston University, Vol. 162, No. 2, 1980.

ISBN 0 909955 35 2

First published March 1981
Reprinted August 1981
Reprinted September 1982
Reprinted June 1983
Reprinted August 1984
Reprinted July 1986
© Primary English Teaching Association
P.O. Box 167, Rozelle, NSW 2039 (818 2591)
Printed in Australia by
Bridge Printery Pty. Ltd.
29-35 Dunning Avenue, Rosebery NSW

Contents

Donald Graves in Australia
Reported by R.D. Walshe

'Children want to write. For years we have underestimated their urge to make marks on paper. We have underestimated that urge because of a lack of understanding of the writing process . . .'

The auditorium is packed. Five hundred pairs of eyes rivet on the stocky man at the lectern. This is Donald Graves of the United States starting a major address on the evening of 19 August 1980 to the Third International English Teaching Conference at Sydney University, Australia.

A journalist would later capture the spirit of that large audience: 'You feel that what he's saying is true. Half-forgotten stirrings of your own 6 year-old self begin to haunt your imagination . .'

They paid him pin-drop attention—punctuated only by bursts of laughter as an expert communicator lightened a serious message with send-ups of adult dullness and pomposity. An hour passed quickly.

'He has the jovial expression, twinkling eyes and rounded head of a genial Friar Tuck,' the journalist continued. 'Graves' spontaneous approach to his research and "his" children is enthusiastic, even passionate.' Then, switching the metaphor, 'He's America's dynamic counterpart to Britain's Mr Chips.'*

An edited version of his Conference address is on page 17—shorn of the magic of the platform presence. It is followed by a selection of articles by Graves and his associates presenting a detailed picture of the work of the University of New Hampshire's 'Writing Process Laboratory', one of America's most talked about educational research enterprises.

I had the pleasure of driving Don Graves around during his fortnight in Sydney, heard him address a dozen meetings, talked with him incessantly. I'd like to pass on what I learned . . .

1. Why We Asked Him to Come

P.E.T.A. specially invited him to the International Conference for two reasons: *first,* because we'd discerned a great upswing of interest since

---

*Laurel Dumbrell, in *Education News* (Canberra), Vol. 17, No. 6, 1981; and *Wombat,* N.S.W. Institute of Technology, October 1980.

1978 in the teaching of writing, in all English-speaking countries but most of all in the United States; *second,* because we'd decided that, world-wide, the most promising research into primary school writing was coming out of the 'Writing Process Laboratory', whose Director was Professor Donald H. Graves. Later, *Time* magazine seemed to confirm our choice by giving top billing to Graves in an article which reported 'a wave of writing reform sweeping the schools, colleges and businesses of the United States' (19 May 1980).

Graves continually uses the term 'the process of writing'. For several years we had realised that the study of *process* is the most fruitful single approach to the teaching and learning of written expression. We located the genesis of the approach in Gordon S. Rohman's 1964 article, 'Pre-writing', which drew lessons from the way professional writers write; Donald M. Murray had extended the idea profoundly in his 1968 book, *A Writer Teaches Writing;* Janet Emig was first to apply it to school writing, in her 1971 research report, *The Composing Processes of Twelfth Graders;* and several later re-searchers had made 'process' studies of the lower secondary grades. Then suddenly there was Donald Graves working with the youngest schoolchildren and proclaiming with missionary zeal that we teachers should 'Let Children Show Us How to Help Them Write' (that being one of many reports from his research 'Laboratory').

So the study of process had begun at the top and was edging down towards the primary school, producing notable changes in the teaching of writing, when Graves went boldly to the *beginnings* of the writing problem. His discoveries will, we are certain, not only greatly improve teaching at this basic level, but influence all later levels of teaching, whether of primary, secondary, tertiary or adult students.

2. The Man Himself

Graves, the man, is interesting. Research into writing is his fifth career; he has also been in the U.S. Coast Guard, a Presbyterian minister-educator, a counsellor, and a teacher-principal. The work at the University of New Hampshire has quickly led to a full professorship. He is an academic who chooses to spend most of his time in classrooms talking with kids and teachers. Socially he is at ease anywhere; never aggressive, but obviously confident of the course he has taken. ('I only report what I have observed.') Talents for humour, metaphor and conversation keep him sanitised against heaviness and jargon, while belief in the flow and variety of *process* prompts him to warn against 'dogmatic naming, classifying, defining'. Questioners at his meetings find that somewhere along the way he has acquired a firm grasp not only of classroom management and English but also of Ed. Psych. and research procedures. Not surprisingly, *Language Arts,* America's leading journal of primary English, has put its 'Research' column in his hands.

He continually throws off ideas whether talking to a crowd or a lunchtime group. Impressive too is his frequent deference to 'My good friend, Don Murray,* the source of many of my ideas.' Fate has happily brought these leading authorities on the process of writing together on the same campus—the two New Hampshire Dons!

He has the mind of the genuine intellectual, continually in creative ferment. Again and again he exclaimed about insights that came to him between talks. 'I'll have to get that down!' he'd say. He meant get it down in 'tomorrow's writing session'. Two acts of daily religious observance are his 5 km jog before breakfast and his half-hour writing session after breakfast. Duties? 'No, I love them both!'

3. New Insight into the Nature of Process

I was to have last-minute benefit of his creativeness. His plane from Melbourne was late, leaving us only an hour for talk at Sydney Airport before he transferred to the flight that would take him home. 'An aborted landing,' he explained. 'Almost hit another plane and had to circle around.' . . . In the airport lounge I raised a key issue: 'How do you meet objections to asking 6 year olds to revise their writing?'

Obviously the question pleased him. Just the day before, he said, he'd had a fresh insight into the forlorn nature of most children's first drafts—and the crucial importance of brightening them by revising.

'Our first reflection on an event is a chaos of impressions,' he said, 'a blur of images, sounds, feelings, words. Take my experience of this aborted landing: my memory of it is at first utterly disordered, yet richly impressionistic. Let's call it the *first* 'rehearsal' of the pre-writing stage of the process. The *second* comes when I really try to select the more important impressions—mostly pictures and phrases and some sequencing of what happened—but, notice, not yet complete sentences and certainly not sentences connected together. Then a *third* 'rehearsal' when I'm strongly working to capture from my stream of "inner speech" full sentences that I might write down—a move from the earlier "telegraphic speech" to what I call "filled-in" speech . . . Notice that all this, so far, is pre-writing. But now, at last, I have a sentence I can write. Down it goes: "The pilot pulled back on the stick because the wheels would not lower and we could not land."

'Imagine how a child feels looking at a bare sentence like that! What has happened to the million rich impressions? Where is the experience that was so significant in one's life? He thinks writing is dumb; it compares so unfavourably with talk . . . And of course it is much worse if he's been asked to write about a topic that is not at all meaningful, being teacher-imposed and outside his experience.

'Well, what has happened is that those several "rehearsals", from rich first *im*pressions to bare and forlorn written *ex*pression, are all increasingly *reductive*—it's a selection process that reduces or distills right down to a core utterance. Now, if we leave writing there, patting the child on the head and saying blandly, "Good, your neatness is

---

*Professor Donald M. Murray is novelist, essayist, teacher of writing, and researcher into the writing process. He is best known in Australia for *A Writer Teaches Writing* (Houghton Mifflin, 1968). He contributed 'Writing as Process: How Writing Finds Its Own Meaning' to *Eight Approaches to Teaching Composition* (NCTE, Illinois, 1980).

improving," then the child will never think well of writing. But if instead we have a "conference" with the child and show interest, ask questions, "What flight was this? When did you first hear something was wrong? How did you feel? . . ." then the child begins to see that something can be done to bring the writing to life, and people will be interested to read it.

'So, after all the reductiveness that produced the first draft, the writer now needs an opposite *development:* building up or elaboration, a serious attempt to capture the most dramatic elements of the first impressions and use them to grip a reader's attention. Revision, redrafting, rewriting—this is what creates real writing. A first draft falls forlornly short of being real writing, and we must allow small children to discover this truth for themselves, most effectively by helping them in one-to-one conferences.'

4. Teaching Writing Is Teaching Craft

'Writing is a craft,' he says, 'and we must teach it as other crafts are taught: in studio or workshop conditions. The pottery teacher doesn't say, Now here's a wheel and here's the clay—*throw!* The writing teacher, like the pottery teacher, must practise the craft alongside the students.'

At his Newcastle meeting he called for professional nudity! . . . 'Writing, real writing, is exposure of inmost thoughts and feelings. When we ask children to write sincerely, we ask them to undress. But they won't do this for long if the teacher never writes, never shows how, never exposes his or her writing to the children—such a teacher has the same effect as the fully dressed visitor to a nudist camp who blunders around gaping at others' nakedness.'

There are many reasons why teachers must write with their children. Writing regularly, they never forget that writing is difficult—for adults as well as children. They know what Dorothy Parker meant when she said, 'I hate writing, but I love having written.' They become sensitive observers of children's writing, moderating their expectations of what children can do at any one drafting. They are continually reminded that writing is not just getting the conventions right but is above all a thinking problem—*what* exactly to say and *how* to arrange it tellingly. And, revealing their own difficulties, they send vital signals to the children: 'I value writing so much that I write myself. You aren't alone in finding it difficult; I do too, but here's how I work to overcome the difficulties. Let's talk about my writing and you might pick up some hints. I'll also tell you what I find the rewards of writing are.'

This needn't mean a heavy burden of writing for the teacher. In fact, no burden at all: 'Write as often as you comfortably can, and try to show as much interest as possible in doing so. But if you can't manage more, then, at the very least, write for five minutes a week with your class.'

5. The Essential Message

'What is the essence of your message?' I asked one day as the car sped towards Wollongong. He replied, typically, in metaphor: 'When people own a place, they look after it; but when it belongs to someone else, they couldn't care less. It's that way with writing. From the first day of school we must leave control of the writing with the child—the choice of topic and the writing itself. Then children write more and care more, even about the appearance of the writing on the page. We teachers must become totally aware of our awful daily temptation to take control away from them, whether by too much prescription or correction or even advice.

'Nothing influences a child's attitude to writing more than the choice of topic. If the child has chosen it and if the teacher shows genuine interest in it, then there's no limit to the effort the child will make. Young children who are given this power soon become confident in choosing topics—not always quick to do so but quite responsible about it, giving the matter deep consideration.

'When their confidence has risen through making many such choices in the area of experience-writing, they become fit to cope with the content subjects, where some prescription of subject matter is necessary. Even then, one hopes, a teacher will not impose a single topic but will rather allow a degree of choice within a broad frame; and this child will know how to work through various options, how to make one of them his topic, and how to limit that topic and set about note-making and writing.'

So central is choice-of-topic-by-the-child to Graves' approach that he has devised special methods for fostering it, methods that appealed to the audiences he addressed*. He hastens to say that of course other ideas are possible. Whatever the method, however, the huge significance of choice-by-the-child is that, at a blow, it dispenses with generalised, teacher-devised topics or lists of topics, substituting *what appeals to each child.*

6. Beginning Writing

'Children want to write . . .' The opening words of Graves' Conference address were simple enough but many teachers would wish to demur. What about the familiar groan that greets announcement of 'Your next composition topic is . . .'?

Here Graves is resolute: 'Our research has established that all children can write at 5-6 years old, can enjoy doing so, and can make at this time *some of the most rapid and delightful growth in writing of their entire lives.* We should look at the system which imposes meaningless topics and not at the children for the reasons why so many are turned off writing.'

Against the 'superstition' that children must learn to read before being allowed to write, he says 90% of children come to school believing they can write, whereas only 15% believe they can read.

---

*See P.E.T.A.'s *P.E.N. 25* for some of these.

A first grade teacher* in the New Hampshire study issued attractively covered writing books to her first-day class of beginners and gently invited them to 'Write!' After grave reflection they all did: a few could already write sentences, some wrote only their names or letters or apparently random words or 'scribble', and some drew a picture. All these forms, if observed with Gravesian perceptiveness, are no less than *beginning levels of understanding and control of self-chosen writing,* and each is the profoundly real base from which a child can take steps forward in writing.

Obviously there are many methods by which children can proceed from here to learn to write. They can learn through a mother's haphazard, play-like demonstrations; or Sylvia Ashton Warner's 'Keywords' scheme; or the Language-Experience school's 'scribing'; or Marie Clay's progression from 'scribble' to print. Donald Graves prefers another approach ('which is as natural as can be')—encouraging children to 'invent their own spellings'. He and his associates in verifying this approach have found that children can write using invented spellings 'so long as we provide them with six consonants, any six.' In a few months many proceed from a single L to represent 'liked' to, e.g., LK — LKT — LOKT — LKET — LIKT — LIKD — LIKED.

'There is no point,' he says, 'in immediately correcting that *L* or *LKT* by writing in the spelling for the child. Too much correction, or correction at the wrong time, can be confusing, not enlightening. Remember, *what you pay attention to, you reinforce.* Premature attention to error, instead of leading to instantly correct spelling, can reinforce a child's self-doubt, so that he decides early he can't spell—he stops trying. But, given time, the natural pressures of the classroom will prompt him to *invent* his way to correct, self-reliant spelling.'

At this early stage, drawing is important to nearly all children. Their tendency is to draw first; it is their means of finding out what they know and what they may write. Beginners respond to a sheet of paper that leaves the top two-thirds for drawing and provides a few widely spaced lines at the bottom for writing. Generally, drawing decreases towards the end of first grade and into second.

Talk too is important. Not, at this stage, 'pre-writing talk' such as conversation with peers or the teacher, though some of that may help, but rather *talking to oneself,* whether audibly or sub-audibly whilst engaging in the hard work of composing. This is 'talk along the way', a small child's necessary verbalising accompaniment of the physical forming of letters and words. To silence it is to stifle writing development. Graves has used sensitive microphones to record this 'mumble' and he reports that it can be 30 to 40 times as abundant as the writing it forges. Not till mid-third grade is it likely to fade away, internalised no doubt as 'inner speech.'

Graves also has a lot to say about what he calls the 'prosodics' of early writing, the signals children devise to point-up the speech

---

* See Mary Ellen Giacobbe's, 'Who Says Children Can't Write the First Week of School?', p. 99; and Susan Sowers' 'KDS CN RIT SUNR THN WE THINGK ', p. 37. N.B. Most U.S. children begin school in first grade at age six.

sounds they consider most important. They might capitalise main nouns, boldly blacken words they want to stress, or use multiple exclamation marks. It is a charming inventiveness and should not be squashed, for they will grow through and out of it—again by about mid-third grade—as they come to realise that written language speaks well enough for itself without extra emphasis in the form of unconventional marks.

7. The 'Conference'

Underlying the stimulating atmosphere of the New Hampshire 'process classrooms' is a simple, powerful interaction that is termed 'the conference': intermittent one-to-one meetings of child and teacher as a piece of writing develops in process. 'We teachers have to learn how to receive a child's fumbling thoughts and writing-in-progress,' says Graves. 'In a conference the child has the salutary experience of finding that someone is interested in what he or she has to say.'

Most children can choose the topic for the next piece of writing from their own continually growing personal list of 'Possible Topics'. But a minority may have difficulty either in choosing the topic or in starting effectively. For this minority the first conference may take place here. The teacher asks questions but does not prompt or prescribe. The child may need to come back with ideas. This is not time lost. It is part of true 'process', basic to leaving control of both topic and writing with the child.

When the child has produced some writing, a conference usually opens with the child telling in a single sentence what the writing is about or what stage it has reached, and then reading the piece aloud, revealing by tone of voice what is valued. Or if the piece is long the teacher might say, 'Read me your most exciting part', and will then listen, understand, asks questions. The interest and the questions elicit creative responses. Again explicit direction is avoided. So is the temptation to make generalised comments like 'Good work' or 'That's interesting'. Instead the questions are specific: 'What will happen next?', 'But why did she get scared?', 'Tell me more about this bit' . . . and again time is allowed for the answers. After some experience, children begin to volunteer ideas for making their writing stronger.

It is difficult to generalise about conferences because each instance is so individual; teachers develop their own styles and try to adapt to each child's need-of-the-moment. 'At the core of the conference,' says Graves, 'is a teacher asking a child to teach her about the subject. The aim is to foster a bursting desire to inform. So the teacher never implies a greater knowledge of this topic than the child possesses, nor treats the child as an inferior learner. We are in the business of *helping children to value what they know*. Ideally, the poorer the writing the greater the interest the teacher will show in it—or rather in what it might become.'

As teachers grow in their ability to receive (or appreciate) children's writing, they become sensitive to what professionals call the 'writer's voice'—the unique personality sounding through the sentences. It becomes possible to detect when this 'voice' is absent or when it breaks down; that is, the point at which the child 'loses control' of the writing, for whatever reason.

The conference is deeply involved with the weightiest issues of writing: purpose, content and style. Graves emphasises, no less, that all the surface mechanics (handwriting, spelling, punctuation) and all the grammar children need to know in primary school can be adequately taught in the conference—at the point of each child's need, instead of through wearisome whole-class exercises.

With children of age 9 or 10 (*very* broadly) Graves sometimes encourages a search for a forceful 'lead'. He likes to see experiment: 'Try writing three or four leads and choose your best.' The 'right lead', a sentence or two, is the one that gets to the heart of the topic, sets up a lively point-of-view, and thrusts the writing into a momentum of sentence-flow.

The case for conferencing, then, is powerful; but teachers often ask, 'How do I do all this one-to-one work in my class of 30?' Graves takes the question very seriously, while pointing out that it is more a problem of classroom management than of writing itself; it involves issues of group work, learning areas, individualisation, and so on.

He instances a classroom where the teacher rosters two groups of four pupils each day: the talking with them usually requires half an hour, an average of 3-4 minutes with each child (though in practice the teacher senses different needs, a minute with one and 10 minutes with another). He has observed many other patterns of classroom organisation and he is writing them up: 'In 1981 I'm assembling our research findings in book form. It won't be narrowly about writing. In fact my present working title is, *Two Crafts: Teaching and Writing.*'

8. The Writing Folder or Collection

'I can't say enough about the importance of the child's Writing Folder,' says Graves. This is the accumulating collection-cum-record of the child's writing. Most of the teachers he works with use two looseleaf folders, one a work-in-progress folder, the other the Folder proper. I heard him urge an audience at the Catholic Education Office to 'Keep every finished piece a child writes. You can't afford to let it go home, because it might not come back, and you would lose a vital part of the record. The whole collection is then available at the school, in the Folder, for the interested parent's inspection.'

The Folder is *valuable for the child* as the visible collection of thoughts expressed, experiences distilled. In a class where writing is valued, the child feels that here is the repository of many of his or her best ideas. It is *valuable for parents* as the best record of the child's progress, the specific progress which cannot be shown in marks or teachers' comments, however conscientious. And it is *valuable for the teacher* as the means of looking back over the year's work to observe development, notice problems, perhaps find reasons for a child's temporary 'writer's block'. Graves says that any teacher who wishes to engage in classroom 'action research' is well advised to mine one or more of the children's folders—there is an infinite amount to be learnt from these records of writing development.

He has his pet format for the Folder: the front-cover carries a Contents, the growing list of topics already written about; the inside-front carries the child's list of topics that might yet be written about (it is continually being added to); and the inside-back carries the child's listing of skills achieved (often noted in conference), expressed in the child's own words, perhaps together with a reference to the piece of writing in which each appeared, not only mechanical skills but whatever the child sees as a new ability. ('I told a joke', 'I used some big words from a book', 'I used speech marks [inverted commas]', etc.).

9. Revision, Rewriting

'Writing only truly becomes writing in revision,' says Graves. 'A professional's first draft is often not much better than anyone else's. It is chiefly in revision that the professional's experience and craftmanship show.'

He has established that children can revise from age five or six. 'Notice how naturally they revise in other media at this age or younger—in block-building, dressing-up, drawing or modelling. True we shouldn't suggest any revision when they're struggling to control the elements of the code; but they soon begin to change a letter or a word, provided we don't hang them up too early on neatness.

'Teachers who are accustomed to imposing topics will say, "My children aren't interested enough to make revisions"—but what they're not interested in is the imposed topic. Revision becomes completely acceptable as they learn to choose their own topics.'

The very young writers, as they move from drawing to scribbling and then to written-down-speech, are guarded from self-criticism and peer-criticism by sheer egocentricity: they write invincibly with lofty indifference to the feelings of others, writing for their own sake. But towards the end of first grade an uncomfortable awareness dawns —readers can be critical or scornful! This can be devastating. The armour of egocentricity is crumpling. Can any new protection be found? In panic the child begins to fear that he can't possibly write well enough to give satisfaction. He confronts inwardly a plethora of thoughts, images and feelings and outwardly all those critical-scornful readers. Suddenly this writing that had seemed easy has become oppressively difficult!

At this period of crisis (which may spread through grades two and three) the troubled young writer needs an understanding teacher —individually, in conference. The child is feeling, 'How can I possibly get enough into my writing to satisfy these readers?' So the teacher helps the child discover additions and make revisions to a threadbare first draft.

Graves says: 'Young writers need to learn a whole repertoire for messing up their first drafts as they change pieces, insert, take out, reorganise. When children stop erasing and instead cross out, draw lines and arrows, or change handwriting from careful printing to a functional scrawl (knowing this to be only a draft) they show awareness that draft writing is temporary, malleable, meant to be changed.'

I reported earlier how Graves had just perceived that the pre-writing 'rehearsal' and then the first draft were *reductive;* slight, bare, rough. So the rest of the writing process—revising and rewriting —must be concerned with injecting the substance and drama and polish that will catch and hold the readers' attention.

This account of Graves' conception of process has so far been *general.* He often pauses, however, to make the point that *every writer has a process as individual as a thumbprint.* The purpose of teaching writing, then, needs to be expressed in properly individual terms: *'We wish to give each child regular opportunities to discover and develop his or her own variety of process and to become confident in applying it to a wide range of writing tasks.'*

The good teacher knows the broad problems that all writers share but is alert to notice the *differences* manifested by young writers as they develop their own individual process. For instance, most will revise several times in their struggle to produce a polished piece for publication, while a few won't be content with less than half a dozen revisions, and there will very occasionally appear a writer who scarcely needs to polish at all, because of an exceptional talent for conceiving and editing writing *in the head* before the pen moves on the page—the rare 'Mozartian' creativity.

10. Audiences and Publication

In stimulating the child to write and to revise, 'publication for a real audience' is no less important to Graves than 'the child's choice of topic' and 'the child's control of the writing'.

Mostly children value the local, immediate audience of teacher and classmates. (Not the teacher only!) Writing and revising in groups guarantees that many eyes inspect the writing at various stages of its development. Occasionally, wider audiences can be specially stimu-lating—parents, the school as a whole, another school, VIPs, etc.

What is publication, in the school sense? Any perusal of a child's writing by any reader at any stage can be considered, broadly, to be publication—and plenty of that elemental kind is built into the ongoing work of a process classroom. But, more formally, a significant part of the children's finished work gets into 'published book form'. The teacher lets it be known that when a child completes 4 or 5 pieces, one can be chosen by the child for publication as a 'book' which will be placed on the classroom or library shelves. Graves reports, for instance, that a first grade class of 22 wrote over a thousand manuscript (MS) books of 1-8 pages in a year and 'published' 420 of them.

'Published' usually means that the child's chosen MS is either typed for the child or carefully handwritten by the child, and then the child illustrates it, staples, tapes or glues it into a 'hard cover', and illustrates the cover. The books usually have a pocket inside the front cover where readers deposit their signed opinions.

'We are accumulating evidence', he says, 'that young children are even more interested in their own and their peers' books than in the printed books from the library. (Though they *do* take out large numbers of books from the library, wishing to see what "other authors" have done.) Certainly this is a marvellous reading resource for any classroom—and cheap! Moreover last year's books are shown to the incoming class and at once they assert a tradition and set a standard.'

11. A Writing Community in the Classroom

While 'conferencing' and other measures stimulate the *individual* writing of every child, the teacher is no less concerned to evolve a *whole class* 'writing community'. 'It adds a learning-force to the teaching-force,' says Graves with a chuckle: 'children learn faster from peer example than from teacher instruction. Have you noticed how they pick up—no, steal!—a good expression or a good idea from a classmate?'

'We are well advised to move swiftly with a new class, getting to know the children really well. By the third week of term we should not only know every child by first name but also his or her main personal interests.* This knowledge is of course our strong base for one-to-one conferences, but it also enables us to encourage partnerships and groups to form, and it guides our choice of class activities, our appeals for materials, and so on. I can usually tell a good writing classroom by the presence of an abundance of children's interests and materials.

'In our rightful concern to individualise, we don't need to overlook whole-class activities like choral recitation or producing a class magazine—activities that build community spirit and complement solo and small group learning. One specifically valuable whole class activity is a daily discussion of three pieces of writing with the class, what we call "a share meeting". It only takes 10 minutes and *it is the writing community deliberating.*'

12. The Centrality of Writing

'Writing is a marvellous unifier', he told a commission of the International Conference. 'We teachers have yet to make proper use of its power in securing the deepest kinds of learning, in improving children's critical thinking, and in integrating the curriculum.'

Later he said, 'Consider any whole piece of original writing done by any child in the junior school: here is the handwriting, spelling, punctuation, grammar and usage that skills-teaching is supposed to be about. But looked at intelligently this piece leaves little need for separate skills teaching. The teacher has only to examine the piece to see what this child needs. Specific help can then be given. This is teaching in context, at the point of need.

See P.E.N. 25 for a method Graves uses to get to know his children.

'It is so much more sensible than whole-class skills exercises. For example, a survey in one school showed that 40% of 6 year olds know how to handle the basic use of inverted commas, so it is obviously a waste of these children's time to keep drilling them in this skill along with the children who don't know.'

Judith Egan, a teacher in the New Hampshire study, was worried about finding enough time for teaching writing effectively—till she grasped that writing need not be taught in isolation. Now she and others have replaced the traditional 'segmented timetable' with a morning session of writing 'out of which all other language activities emerge'. Invariably they find that, not only do the children write and draw keenly, but their reading-test results improve, there is an abundance of purposeful talking and listening, all the language work is admirably integrated, and every day brings a new crop of unpredictable but creative happenings which enable the teacher to branch in any desired direction. Moreover spelling, handwriting and the conventions get all the attention they need. And, of key importance, the children are regularly experiencing the *process* of drawing/drafting/revising/rewriting/publishing.

The hour at the airport sped by.

'That's the second call for your flight,' I said.

'What can I say at parting?' he mused. 'So many marvellous audiences, so much interest—and yet the process approach will need a long struggle to get it to the mass level. Sometimes I'm daunted by the inertia.'

I fumbled for something reassuring: 'What we're trying to change has been going on for 2500 years—since the Greeks—the crazy notion that you've got to get your writing right in the first draft or you're a failure, you can't write. It's no wonder generations of kids have decided they can't write, they hate writing.'

'Yes,' he said, 'and only the regular practising of the process will help them realise that not even the professionals can get it right straight off. Everyone needs to revise and everyone *can* revise—and that means *everyone can learn to write,* at least competently. It would put an end to all this fear of writing . . . Oh, well, I do hope P.E.T.A. thinks the trip has been worthwhile?'

'We can't add to what James Britton said at the end of your Strathfield meeting. I heard him. He strode right to the front and said, "Donald, that was smashing!" and we feel like that about your whole trip.'

'Jimmy is so generous!' . . . the Friar Tuck smile again, and 'Let's keep in touch. I'd love to get back—so many Australian friends!' . . . and he was gone through the impersonal doors of the Customs check.

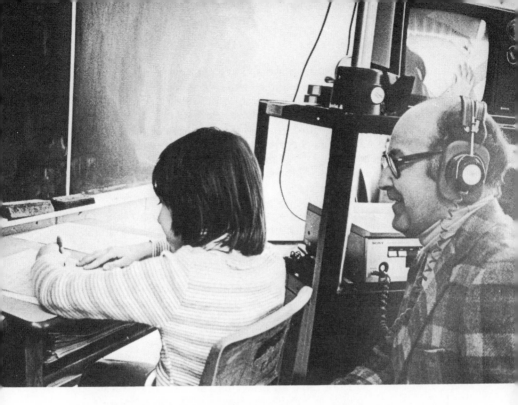

1. Patterns of Child Control of the Writing Process*

Donald H. Graves

CHILDREN WANT TO WRITE. For years we have underestimated their urge to make marks on paper. We have underestimated that urge because of a lack of understanding of the writing process, and what children do in order to control it. Without realising it we wrest control away from the children and place road blocks that thwart their intentions. Then we say, 'They don't want to write. What is a good way to motivate them?'

Children show us how they seek to control writing when they go about composing. They show us their stumbling blocks and the orders in which they grow in the writing process. They don't show with any one behaviour, nor in an antiseptic laboratory setting. Rather, they show us their growth patterns over a long period of time and in the setting where they normally function, the classroom. If we are going to help children, and not stand in the way of their gaining control of their own writing, we need to become familiar with what they do when they write. This evening I will report on two areas of data from our two year study of how children gain control of the writing process, 'Children's Transitions from Oral to Written Discourse' and 'Children's Development in Revision'.

*Address to the Third International Conference on the Teaching of English, Sydney, Australia, 19 August, 1980.

Three researchers, Susan Sowers, Lucy Calkins and I, have just completed two years observing sixteen children in a small rural school in new Hampshire, U.S.A. The sixteen children were chosen because of their differences in ability. Some hardly knew how to hold a pencil in first grade whereas some third graders were capable of writing eight to ten pages of a story. The children were followed in two clusters: (1) grades one through two and (2) grades three through four. In this way we were able to map how children grew in control of the writing process over the first four years of school.

The sixteen children were observed directly in the classroom. That is, we did not gather information unless the teacher asked the children to write or the child chose to write. Information was gathered by hand recording or video taping child behaviours during the writing process. We also used interviews, structured interventions, and the analysis of children's writings. Everything that the children wrote in any subject area was xeroxed during the two years. In the main, the researchers attempted to gain information with the least interference to the children.

Still, we bear no illusions. The presence of the researchers had great influence. It is impossible to have three guests in a home for two years, every day, and not have an effect on the owners or residents. We had a specific policy of not conducting workshops with staff, or consciously seeking to change teacher direction. We had this policy because we wanted to be good guests. If teachers, administrators, or parents wanted to ask about what we we were doing, we would be happy to answer, or share our data on request. My suspicion is, that because we took this stance, we had many more professional-type questions than might ordinarily be expected. In a way, we ended up having more influence on environment than might be expected.

In spite of this influence we did not feel our objectives would be lost — that is, determining how children would grow in their control of the writing process. Our theory (and I believe the data holds us up) was that if teachers were comfortable with the teaching of writing, knew more about it, and responded effectively to the children, a wider range of development would ensue. In turn, we would gather more information. Furthermore, the *order of development would not be changed,* the order of problems solved would be basically unchanged, even though the rate of solution might be accelerated.

Since our research was designed to find out 'what' was involved in the growth of children's control of the writing process, more than 'why', we felt secure with this arrangement. One other very helpful outcome of this approach to research was that teachers themselves became collaborators in the research project. Since they maintained control of their teaching they became quite aggressive in stating their opinions about writing and the research data. Major contributions were made by the teachers. On countless occasions they had indispensable observations and records on the children.

Making the Transition from Speech to Print

There is much for children to learn to control in writing that is very different than speech. They must supply the context, write in a certain direction, learn to control the space-time dimensions of writing on a flat surface, understand what the medium of writing can do, know the relation between sound and symbols, know how to make the symbols, learn to put symbols in a particular order, and while composing one operation understand its relation to the entire order of what has been and will be in the message and compose in a medium where the audience is not usually present.

When children first write they are fearless. Egocentricity has its own protective cloak. Children are merely concerned with getting the marks on the paper and usually getting it down for themselves. Children are quite pleased with their own competence and they experiment fearlessly with the new medium given a small amount of encouragement. Although children share work with others, this work is usually done for themselves. The behaviours displayed during writing are very similar to other play behaviours. Fortunately children are not aware of all the transition steps they are making from speech to print. The child is a delightful pragmatist and seems to be saying, 'I want to get this writing down. I'm doing it because I want to and what I am putting down is not only interesting to me but to others as well'.

Children's attempts to control the conventions of writing are marked by many holdovers from speech. For example, in speaking, the context is usually supplied by the parties to the communication. Charles and Edward are working in the block area and Charles wants Edward's curved block. Charles merely points to the curved block and says, 'Give me that one'. But when Charles writes he must provide the setting through the words he supplies. Charles doesn't know how to provide the setting, the context for his writing. Instinctively he does much of this through drawing before he writes. The drawing provides double duty. On the one hand it provides the setting for the text, on the other it serves as a rehearsal for what he will write.

Although speech is directional, compared to the specifics of letter following letter on the printed page, it is non-directional. When children first write, their messages go in many directions. They may start in the middle, lower right, or upper left of the page and proceed in column form or diagonally, depending on the whim of the writer. If the child is aware of word separation, words may follow in column form, looping diagonals, even in a circle. In either case the child is aware that letters follow letters. Breaks for words are done by more advanced writers, again reflecting a written feature, since most words are run together in conversation — as do most words first written by the children.

Teachers permit most of the first grade children in our study to learn spelling via spelling inventions. That is, the child spells the word the way it sounds. Thus, from the first day children are able to use whatever sound-symbol relationships they know to produce messages. At this point it appears that a child who knows six sound-symbol relationships (usually consonants) can begin to write. And they do. This year on the first day of school Mrs Giacobbe, one of the first grade teachers, passed out bound, hard-covered books with the child's name in embossed letters on the outside. She merely said, 'Write'. Even though thirty percent of the children had had no preschool experience they all wrote in their fashion. Some drew, others wrote their names, some put down numbers and letters, and about five wrote in sentences. The important thing is that none of the children believed they couldn't write.

Spelling inventions make it possible for children to control their messages from the first day of school. In addition, our data show that the words evolve from crude spellings to greater refinement. Susan Sowers, research associate on the project, has taken all words used by different cases, traced and dated their spelling evolutions during their first year in the study. The following is an example of a word tracing:

Toni's Pattern			*Sarah's Pattern*		
11/10 — LC	— Like		11/20 — FLLAOWZ	— flowers
LAT	— liked		FLLAWRZ	
12/8 — LOCT	— liked		FLLAWR	— flower
12/19 — L	— like		1/11 — FLAWRS	
4/10 — LICT	— liked		6/1 — FLOWERS	
KLIC	— like			
5/14 — LIKE				
5/21 — LIKE				

At first the children feel little control since they know too few sound-symbol relationships to provide enough cues to recognise it again. Toni's 'LC' or 'L' above for *like* may be difficult to read at a later time. On the other hand 'LICT' gives more cues. It is an important moment when the child is able to compose, and read back his information from the page. In several instances we were able to be present with our video cameras when the child first realised he had the power to read his own message. 'I don't know how I do-ed that,' one child said.

Putting symbols in order is a difficult task for many children. The ordering of symbols is quite dependent on the speed with which a child recognises sound-symbol relationships from his own speech and the speed with which the letter is written. Sometimes the process is so slowed down by the difficulty the child has in retrieving the letter unit from his own speech that the full context of the message is lost. In figure 1, notice how Jamie makes sounds to produce the correct sound-symbol relationship, yet must continually reorient himself to where he is in the message. Jamie produces the message so slowly that the text is obliterated by the next sound-symbol he encounters. He then must reread from the beginning each time in order to add the new letter in a word. The first line in figure 1 indicates the point at which the letter was written in relation to the second line, the sounds produced by the child.

Figure 1 shows just how much language and sound Jamie must produce to sequence the letters for his message, 'A tornado went by here now'. It took him fifteen minutes to write his *unassigned*

Figure 1: Jamie's Composing

WRITING LINE 𝒜   𝒳 𝒩

SOUND LINE   T   T   T   N   Ae tonaido   D   D   D

                          erases

COMMENT LINE   M   (tornado)

                    makes an
                       N

WRITING LINE 𝒟   𝒜

SOUND LINE   D D Ae tonaido Ae oo au Ae To na do

COMMENT LINE Stops to
              check letter
              chart

message. How easy it is to assume that Jamie struggles because he must produce a product. Jamie doesn't know he is supposed to be having difficulty. Jamie had just seen an account of a tornado's destruction on television and wanted to write about it. Jamie wrote this message in December at the bottom of a drawing he had already composed on tornados. Note how few cues are in this message for Jamie to read. In fact, he could not read the sentence, only 'tornado'.

Most young writers who make the transition from oral to written discourse must produce language and sound when they write. The following are some of the different types recorded thus far from our video transcripts:

1. *Sounding* to probe for sound-symbol relation.
2. *Sounding* to 'break off' a phonemic unit from the word under attack.
3. *Rereading language* for reorientation in the composing unit. The child must hear where he is in the text. The difficulty or length of time spent on the composing operation determines how much the writer must reread.
4. *Conversations with friends:* 'This monster is going to eat up all the good guys'.
5. *Procedural language:* 'Now what am I going to do? No, this isn't right. I need to change it.' Procedural language is a more advanced form of transition from speech to print.
6. *Advanced statement of the text:* The child says the text in order to sense the appropriateness of the current word. 'He *cast* the line into the stream.' The child is now writing 'cast' but wants to make sure it fits correctly into the rest of sentence. This is very different from Jamie who has to say everything *before* the current operation. 'A tornado come *by.*' 'By' is the word under draft but is determined syntactically by all that has preceded it, not by what may lie ahead.

7. *Conversations before and after the composing:* Not only is the child speaking during the composing, but language surrounds the entire written event. *Before:* 'I'm going to write about monsters today. And you know what, the good guys are going to lose.' *After:* 'I'm finished, Mrs Giacobbe, and everybody's killed. Look at 'em here, all burned up. See, this ray gun (pointing to the picture, not the text) cooked every one of 'em.'

In summary, the amount of language a child must produce before, during and after the written event is paramount. Beginning writers show through voice alone that writing is much more of a *speech* event than a writing event. A careful assessment of the nature of language the child supplies also gives us a picture of where the child is in his control of the writing process. These are data that make it possible for the teacher to help the child gain, and maintain control of his own writing.

As children gain more distance on the writing process they deal with new issues in making the transition from speech to print. Children speak less, make fewer vocalisations, and show more prosodics in their writing. That is, more speech forms appear in the writing. Ask the child to read while you observe his paper. The child will show with his voice how he uses prosodics. Examples of some of the prosodics are the following:

> capitalisation of important words — 'Jumped'
> capitalisation of the entire word — 'The fish BIT!'
> blackening in important words, capitalisations
> underlining important words.

Children also place more sound in their text through the use of interjections, dialogue, and exclamation marks.

These features enter texts toward the end of the first grade. They come at a point when children grow in audience sense, gain skill in reading, and become interested in conventions. All three of these factors seem to occur simultaneously. They are accompanied by child statements that show distance, yet show a disturbance about their new lack of control in composing: 'This is stupid. This isn't what I want. I used to be able to write good, but I can't anymore. I don't like the sound of this.'

Later as children gain more control of their information, realise that the data are strong enough to support themselves without prosodic markers, the markers fade. At this point children have usually moved into much more advanced uses of revision, sustaining a single selection over several weeks. New levels of control have been reached. The child writes to find out more what he means. The writing, as we shall see in Lucy Calkins data on revision, becomes clay, is malleable, and doesn't need such explicit speech markers.

Summary of Principles. A number of principles emerge in reviewing how children gain control of making the transition from speaking to writing:

- At first children need to hear and see what they mean. They control their writing through drawing and speaking as they write, and in discussing the writing with friends and the teacher. Writing is more speech than writing.
- As children gain distance on the process of relating sounds to symbols, and handwriting issues are put behind them, they become more dissatisfied with their text and look for new ways to insert speech features.
- At first writing is a highly egocentric exercise. Later, as the child gains more distance on the text and other children provide different responses, he realises the message needs to be changed.

Children's Development in Revision

When children revise they demonstrate their changing visions of information, levels of thinking, what problems they are solving, and their level of control over the writing process. Revision is not only an important tool in a writer's repertoire, but is one of the best indices of how children change as writers. For this reason, the data on revision has been one of the most important aspects of our study of children's writing.

Consistent with transitions from speech to print, children first revise their drawings because the drawings are more important. If children feel their drawing is accurate, the text is seldom changed. Simple changes in syntactical accuracy, changing words because of the way they are formed on the page, or the addition of words for the sake of feeling are typical of first revisions.

At first children write for the sake of writing. They enjoy putting marks on paper. Their composing behaviours are play-like. The decision to write, the composing and completion of a selection may all occur in the space of ten to fifteen minutes. The child does not look back. Attempts to 'revise' the completed work with the child are sometimes met with diffidence or polite participation. The concept of the work as a message, usable at another place and time, is not necessarily understood by the child.

For this reason it is all the more important for the teacher to 'revisit' the writing through the give and take of an oral conference. The conference becomes the bridge between past and present in which the child gains distance on the content and the concept of what writing can do. Furthermore, the conference is an invaluable source of information for both the teacher and child. Conferences run from three to twenty minutes. Transcripts of hundreds of teacher-child conferences over the two year period have given us a valuable profile of the child's control of the writing process. Barbara Kamler of Riverina College at Wagga Wagga, who just spent six months with us at the research site, has written a very important article* for the September issue of *Language Arts* (NCTE), in which she documents myriads of influences on one child's written selection as it developed

---

*The article is reproduced on p. 73 of the present book.—*Ed.*

over a two to three week period. Her work closely documents the many functions of the language conference through actual transcripts between teacher and child and the child with other children.

The language conference that focuses on the child's paper is the cornerstone of children's revision. As the teacher revisits the child's paper, listens to the voice of the child as the paper is read, or notices the child's uneasiness about some information, the seeds of the child's desire to revise are observed.

Children wish the new information were in the text when they have chosen a topic that they feel is an important one in their own lives, one worth publishing, one containing information of interest to other children, or one that is of great length. When these first grade children 'revise', the revision is usually in the form of adding information at the beginning or end of the selection. Seldom does it occur in the interior of the text. Disturbing the interior of the text is much more sophisticated than dealing with initial and final states.

Even though the strength of the topic is a strong determinant in the child's interest in revision, several other factors are involved. First, the child needs to spell and write comfortably, having enough speed so that extra writing does not become a penalty. Second, the child must have help in dealing with some of the effects of his first experiences with audience. Third, the child gets help in dealing with spatial-aesthetic issues of changing the text.

When children have sufficient speed in the motor, sound-symbol components, and the general ordering of these on the page, the child can attend more to the text. No longer is the child losing sense of syntax because of the demands of spelling and letter formation. Now when the child is asked, 'And then what will happen?', the child is able to answer several sentences ahead, whereas before, the child was unable to think beyond the next word. In short, the child is now operating in a much broader space-time frame on the text and can have greater distance on the information.

With distance the child does not find freedom. New problems of control arise. The child can usually read well enough now to recognise the discrepancy between intentions and what, in fact, has occurred in the text. The child does not necessarily like what he sees. Up to this time egocentricity has provided a protective mask, pushing the child into playful activity when writing. Audiences may have responded negatively to what he has done, but the child does not hear. He believes the audience has major problems. *He* does not.

At the end of their first formal year of schooling, many children shed their egocentric masks. When they do, they are not unlike the butterfly emerging from the chrysalis: weak, floppy, grotesque in movement, yet full of promise. They begin to hear the comments of classmates and teachers. They are aware of a discrepancy between their intentions and what is on the paper. 'It doesn't sound good,' says the child. The child wants to change the selection but often doesn't know how. Children may cease to write, avoid writing, or turn to the stronger suit of reading. For many young writers this is a highly vulnerable time, one that calls for an understanding teacher in conferences, a teacher who has helped the class to become a good audience. More than ever, a teacher's comments need to be specific, carefully listening to the child's voice as the paper is discussed.

A third element that stands in the way of children's control of revision at this time is the spatial-aesthetic issue. Children simply don't know how to fit in the new information. The teacher may say, 'Show me where you want to put what you have just said. The child may not be able to locate where the information should go. If the child can locate it, he may still not know the mechanics of inserting information. Writing up margins, drawing arrows, putting in a caret are not tools that are part of the child's repertoire. Up to this point most of the children have erased words or several sentences when changes were made. But looking through the child's eyes, this question arises, 'How do you put something in when you don't want to change what's already there?' Splicing is new territory. The child needs help.

Revision presents an aesthetic barrier. The reason most children erase is to preserve the appearance of the paper. This occurs even in rooms where teachers stress lining out, or drawing arrows as a revising procedure. Children erase because they want the next to be right the first time.

Have you ever observed children during the moment of their first encounter with a new piece of blank paper? Note how many times they 'clean' it before writing on it. They stroke, brush, even blow away imaginary dust. The cleaning continues during and after writing as well.

The following writing conference demonstrates a child in transition and how the teacher helped him deal with the spatial-aesthetic issues:

Teacher: I see that you were able to put in the word 'may' to show that 'Brontosaurus *may* travel in families'. (Chris had been able to sandwich in the small word without erasing.) But you didn't say why they travel in families.

Chris: They travel in families to protect the young.

Teacher: Do you think that is important information?

Chris: Yes, but there isn't any place to put it. (Chris's writing goes from left to right over to the right hand margin at the bottom of the paper. Above this writing is a picture of a brontosaurus.)

Teacher: Look the paper over and show me where you could write it in.

Chris: There isn't any . . . (voice rising)

Teacher: Look the entire paper over and put your hand on any space where there isn't writing or drawing. (There is a space above the drawing.)

Chris: Well, I could put it up here (motions to the top of the paper) but it would look stupid. The other part is down here.

Teacher: How could you show they were connected?

Chris: I could put an arrow down here pointing to the part that's at the top.

Teacher: Good, but you'll need to connect the arrow with the top. This is what writers do when they are getting their books ready for the publisher.

What doesn't show in the dialogue is Chris's concern about drawing the line connecting the information from the bottom to the top. Although he came up with the solution for the placement of information, he was not satisfied with the appearance of the product. He was pleased to know what professional writers would do when they wrote, but still may wish to recopy the text.

Revision in the Upper Primary Grades. Lucy McCormick Calkins, research associate on this study, has completed a major work on revision practices of third grade children. She has identified four kinds of revisers from observation of child behaviours during writing, the analysis of their drafts, and data gathered from their attempts to revise a text written by Calkins about a common classroom experience. In the last of these, the children were directed to revise a text filled with informational inaccuracies. They first told the researcher what they felt should be changed. Then they changed the text on the page they had just critiqued.

Calkins has particularly attended to how children change their use of information when revising. She asks such questions as: 'How does the information change between first and last drafts? When children move from one draft to another, how do they use the last draft when they compose the new one? What are the changing strategies that children use as they advance in the writing process?' Her report of this phase of our study will appear in the fall issue of *Research in the Teaching of English* (NCTE).

Calkins found that children's strategies followed time-space development in a very consistent way. The degree to which they were able to control revision was dependent on their ability to use the draft from one page to the next, their ability to infuse information into the text, then to manipulate information from one page to another. These abilities show in the practices of the four types of revisers:

TYPE I These children write successive drafts without looking back to earlier drafts. Because they do not reread and reconsider what they have written, there is no comparison or weighing of options. Changes between drafts seem arbitrary. Rewriting appears to be a random, undirected process of continually moving on. In their own writing they have many unfinished writing selections. They learn little from draft to draft. On the common classroom exercise, they might come up with new information but could only add it on to the end of selections.

TYPE II These children keep refining earlier work but the refinement is of minor consequence. The content and structure of their writing does not change. Some spelling, punctuation, or a word or two might be changed, but that is all. On the common classroom exercise, these children, unlike *Type I* children, would look back at the text and come up with new information, but could not insert the data in the text.

TYPE III These children move between periods when they refine drafts and periods when they are continually abandoning them and beginning new ones. At times they appear to be like *Type I* children, but they are closer to being *Type II* children. Moreover, their periods of restless discontent with their drafts indicate that they are in transition to the next level, *Type IV*. On the common classroom exercise, they are able to insert the information convincingly into the text. Their restlessness seems to come from the higher standards they have set themselves.

TYPE IV For these children, revision results from interaction between writer and draft, between writer and internalised audience, between writer and evolving subject. They reread to see what they have said and to discover what they want to say. There is a constant vying between intended meaning and discovered meaning, between the forward motion of making and the backward motion of assessing. On the common classroom exercise, these children immediately asked if they could change parts of it. One change led to another. Arrows, lines, stars and carets were used to change and insert the information.

Most writers seem to go through these four stages of development in revision. More data will be added, findings of the first year checked from another entire year of information on revision. Without extensive review of the data, many children have advanced in stages of revision. Many of the type IV children from the third grade have changed drafting habits—that is, they no longer do as many drafts, and more information appears in final draft form from the first draft. They also do more rehearsing of writing when they are not in class. They think about revision strategies when they are with friends or reading or watching television.

Lest all of these revision data sound too cut and dried, it is important to mention one child, Amy, who does not fit this pattern of development. Amy was a good writer from the start of the study but did not revise. She was the kind of child who would sit down to write and produce the following lead about cheetahs: 'A cheetah would make a sports car look like a turtle'. Her first drafts were better than most of the *Type IV* children who did extensive revisions. For a year and a half Amy baffled us both with the quality of her writing and her lack of revisions. Amy could tell by our questions that we didn't understand how she went about composing. I think she enjoyed our perplexity.

In April of this year she informed Lucy Calkins:

> I think I know how I write. The other night I was lying in bed and I couldn't get to sleep. I was thinking, 'I wonder how I will start my fox piece in the morning'. It was 9:30 at night and Sidney my cat was next to me on the bed. I thought and thought and couldn't figure how to start it. Finally, about 10:30, my sister came home and she turned on the hall light. Now my door has a round hole where there ought to be a lock. A beam of light came through the hole and struck Sidney in the face. Sidney went 'squint'. Then I knew how I would start my fox piece:

'There was a fox who lived in a den and over the den was a stump and in the stump was a crack and a beam of light came through the crack and struck the fox full in the face.'

Amy is an excellent artist with an eye for detail and the language to go with what she sees. She does many off-stage rehearsals of what she will write. From this incident we merely get a glimpse of what she must do as she goes her own way in composing. Fortunately she has a teacher who does not assign revisions just for the sake of revision.

Final Reflection

These data on children's transition from speech to print and on the process of revision provide a base for observing children as they change in the writing process. These data are not cast in concrete. They must be viewed within the limitation of the setting in which they were gathered. I think the data show us *what ingredients* are significant in observing children's growth as writers.

I am frequently asked, 'What can I do to speed up children's growth as writers? What can I do as a teacher to move the child from a *Type I* to a *Type IV* writer?' It is natural to want children to progress. But our anxieties about child growth lead us to take control of the writing away from the children. We want to produce materials or come up with methods that unfortunately convince children that the source of control of their writing lies outside of themselves. When children feel in control of their writing their dedication is such that they violate the child labour laws. We could never assign what they choose to do.

The teachers at our site have taught me a great deal in these two years of inservice training for researchers. They have slowed the process of teaching down in such a way that children have begun to catch up to what they already know. They listen for children's intentions to emerge, observe where they are in their development, and then find ways to provide the appointment for the child to control what he is doing.

Children will continually surprise us if we let them. As in Amy's case, when everyone seems to fit a pattern, if we look carefully, many do not. This may seem to lessen the importance of growth patterns across children. I think it heightens their importance. They are a solid base from which we can see the important differences in each child. And every child has them. As the study has gone on, we have become more fascinated with the differences in children than in their similarities. This is what happens when we slow down, listen, and let the children lead. That is the joy of both research and teaching.

2. The Researcher Who Watches Children Write

Susan Sowers

'HERE'S YOUR BACON BURGER, DR GRAVES,' Chris says to the man with the clipboard at the first grade math area. The children count and solve arithmetic problems with miniature bacon, eggs, strawberries, and brown and white cookies. Chris has turned it into a restaurant.

'I don't see a bacon burger on the menu. Is this something that is not on the menu?' Graves asks. Chris goes to get paper and a stapler.

Graves, a bald, middle-aged professor, sits with surprising ease on a chair whose tiny seat is twelve inches above the floor. Chris has brown hair and a missing front tooth. He has won his classmates' admiration for his lively plans and games, but their bids for his approval of a clay submarine and a skyscraper in blocks don't delay him long.

'Tusdays special,' the seven-year-old writes on a small square of paper. On another he writes, 'apple soup' and 'Todays special Bacon Burger.'

'You know, taxes are going up, too,' says Chris. He staples the specials to the menu he had written yesterday.

'Now, what do you want to eat?' Chris asks.

'I'd like a bacon burger and a cup of coffee, but I don't see any coffee on the menu.'

Chris adds coffee. 'Would you like an appetiser? How about strawberries?'

Graves quizzes him on the price of strawberries before he agrees to order them as an appetiser.

'OK,' Graves says, 'how much will all this cost?'

'The coffee and appetiser go with the meal. It will all cost one dollar,' says Chris.

'How do I pay for all of this?' Graves asks.

'Write a cheque.'

Graves hands his cheque to Chris. '"Pay to the order of Snack Place. One dollar and no cents. D.H. Graves,"' Chris reads with hesitation.

When Mrs Giacobbe's first grade class goes to lunch, Graves takes Chris's menu from his cubby and the stories that Laura, Ann, and Shannon had written that morning to xerox at the school office.

Chris's customer at Snack Place is Professor Donald H. Graves of the University of New Hampshire. Chris is one of sixteen children Graves and his research associates Lucy Calkins and Susan Sowers will observe for the next two years to learn how children change in their writing processes. The writing process is new territory in research which Graves' award-winning doctoral dissertation in 1973 helped to open.

Graves stopped in the teachers' room to tell Mary Ellen Giacobbe, who had been too busy with a group of children to overhear, and Jean Robbins, the principal, about his conversation with Chris. He talked with his hands and laughed with the delight he had suppressed while talking to Chris.

'Then I said to Chris, "Isn't ten cents awfully cheap for strawberries this time of year? How can you make a profit?"

'And he said, "It's alright. We raise our own strawberries."

'"But what about the cost of fertiliser and your own labor?" I said.

'"We don't buy fertiliser. We do it the natural way," he told me.

'"What about the cost of plants?" But I couldn't stump him!

'"We had to buy plants the first year. Strawberry plants send out runners with new plants, so we don't have to buy any more."'

Giacobbe, Robbins, and the other teachers shook their heads with astonishment and laughed with Graves at seven-year-old Chris's wide knowledge and unshakable poise.

Graves chose Atkinson Academy as the site for his study because Robbins and her staff are an open, cooperative group of professionals who are genuinely interested in helping children. Most important, children *do* write at Atkinson. Grammar exercises are not accepted as a substitute as is the case in more and more schools.

A brass plaque in front of Atkinson Academy states that it was built in 1803. Although 'Academy' is part of its name, the school serves Atkinson, New Hampshire, formerly a small New England town and now a bedroom community for Boston commuters.

The oldest part of the building has two classrooms on each of its two floors. The roof is topped by a cupola. The flagpole that extends from the second storey is not aluminum but a thin, nearly-straight wooden pole. Like many old houses in New England towns, Atkinson Academy grew because its later occupants needed more space and built several additions behind the original white wooden building.

About a quarter of a mile down the road past the Atkinson Grange and a few houses stands Rockwell, a brick building that houses three more classrooms. Graves and his research associates follow children in two classrooms at Rockwell and three in the main building.

Chris is not a typical first grade child. He, like the other fifteen children in the first and third grades, was not chosen at random to be the subject of an experiment. Chris was selected for his unique characteristics. He is a very bright, developmentally advanced first grade boy. Graves and Calkins observed the five classes for several weeks before deciding which children would provide the most data at different levels of development—advanced, average, and slow—in the first and third grades.

Graves' use of the case study method includes close observation and interviews. His conversation with Chris in the restaurant was an exploration. While Chris wrote, Graves recorded what he said and did in a double column form which he designed in a previous study:

Words Written by Child			*Observer Comments*
Tusdays Sp	ecial		(2) Writes 'sp' quickly.
(1)	(2)	(3)	
			(3) Chris: 'How do you spell special?' Spelling is given.
apple	soup		(4) Chris comments, 'You know, taxes are going up, too.'
(4)	(5)	(6)	
			(5) Chris: 'How do you spell soup?' Researcher: 'You know how to spell that word.' Chris writes.
			(6) Chris takes this writing, done on coloured paper about 4″ x 4″, and staples the 'special' to main menu.
Todays Special			(7) Voices as he writes Todays.
(7)	(8)		(8) Copies 'Special' from word written on previous ticket. Makes several trips to get it right.
Bacon burger			(10) Writes and sounds two letters at a time when he copies this word from the other menu.
(9)	(10)		
			(11) Chris: 'What do you want to eat?' Researcher: 'I'd like a bacon burger and a cup of coffee, but I don't see any coffee on the menu.'
coffee			
(12)	(13)	(14)	(12) Chris writes 'coffee' on main menu.

(13) Chris: 'Would you like an appetiser?
How about strawberries?'
Researcher: 'OK'.

(14) Researcher: 'How much will all this
cost?' Chris: 'The coffee and
appetiser go with the meal. It will all
cost one dollar.'

This writing episode, when placed beside others that precede it
and follow it will show changes in Chris's writing process. For
instance, Chris used resources four times in his nine-word episode:
twice, in 3 and 5, he asked Graves for a spelling word; and twice, in 8
and 10, he referred to words already written. Chris voiced the words
as he wrote or sounded the letters in 7 and 10. Chris's behaviour in the
writing process occupies Graves' attention far more than the written
product with accidents such as a missing apostrophe and misspelling
in 'Tusday'.

Chris's behaviour shows that he knows a lot about restaurants —
the way menus and specials are displayed, a single price for the meal,
appetiser, and coffee incidentally avoiding the problems of adding up
a cheque, and knowing that people can pay with cheques. His
comment on taxes, 'You know, taxes are going up, too,' is certainly
appropriate for a proprietor of a small restaurant whether he means
his property taxes or that food, too, is rising in price.

After recording Chris's play and writing at The Snack Place,
Graves summarised his observations: 'Chris is widening his writing
vocabulary through the store. He has an excellent understanding of
meal components. The attachments as special tickets to the main
menu are quite sophisticated, especially his use of the word appetiser.

'About five minutes later—after the researcher had left—I
overheard Chris say to Allen, "I'm sick of this, let's do something else."

'Note: Chris ends highly involved episodes abruptly. When things
are done, they are *done*. This still indicates that Chris does things for
the *doing;* they are ends in themselves, not necessarily for use at
another time, although he did use yesterday's menu, and the study of
whales has gone on for at least a week and one half. An issue:
transitions.'

Graves' summary shows Chris's writing in the context of other
events. In the prewriting or rehearsal stage, Chris learned about
restaurants, taxes, and how strawberries grow. He played restaurant
in the math area the day before. As Graves observed, Chris writes for
the moment. An audience distant in time and space is not yet
important to Chris. When it is, he will begin to revise and edit — the
third stage of the writing process.

Each influence in Chris' writing is a variable. In his proposal to
the National Institute of Education for funding for the two-year
project, Graves listed thirty-five variables that he hoped to follow in
the study: '... the purpose of case study investigation is to locate new
variables. Previous experience with two other case study

investigations shows that half again as many new questions or variables are uncovered,' he wrote in the proposal.

To show the importance of case study research, Graves cites Piaget's breakthroughs studying his own three children and Dr John Laragh's case study research leading to advances in treating hypertension. 'But the work has to be meticulous and done over time,' Graves warns. 'When a child took the Binet (an I.Q. test) and gave all the wrong answers, Piaget asked, "Why did he do that?" Every piece of information is information. If the child does something unpredictable, happy day! In teaching we can't be threatened. We ask, "What are we going to do with that?"

'It's presumptuous to make statements about how children develop without observation. Ken Goodman and Yetta Goodman got to know kids. They could see why they were reading the way they were reading. Observation leads to being responsive. They have a way of caring about children. Their research model was a responsive model which leads to responsive teaching. We've had so much unresponsive research. I hope research might be compatible with the way in which findings might be carried out.'

Graves' knowledge of children showed research associate Calkins what children struggle with. After the first day observing the children she said, 'I went into one room where all the children were copying from page 213 of their math books. I walked around the room wondering, 'What am I supposed to do here?' I noticed that some added the hundreds column before the tens and ones. I shifted my weight and looked around and wondered if that was what I'm supposed to see.

'Then I talked to Don [Graves] about the room in the car on the way back. He was excited. "Wasn't that incredible?" he said. He'd noticed so much about the children that I'd missed. He said, "Did you see how one child sat on a short chair at a high table and was writing math problems at armpit level? Did you notice the angles of the papers to the children's bodies? Think how that changes their perspective on the math book and what that does to copying and writing. Some children had to voice the problems in order to write them, and some had to look at the book, write a digit, look back for the next digit, write it, find their place in the book and so forth until they copied the problem one digit at a time." He even noticed the pencils. One child wrote with a stubby pencil which made his writing small and cramped.'

Graves' ability to help teachers see children only begins with conversations. He writes about his research so that other will see what children do, too. Here is his description of the child whom he observed for his doctoral dissertation:

> I was startled by the sound of machine gun fire from the rear. Quickly I turned . . . and noted that seven-year-old Michael was writing again. He would gaze at his drawing of warfare between Germans and Americans at the top of his paper, reach up and crayon in a red explosion for emphasis, and with shooting noises escaping from his lips return to the written description of his private war. Although classified

as a reader at the pre-primer level, Michael struggled with an average of three unassigned writings per day, yet apparently enjoyed the full process of writing.

Graves loves to tell stories. 'Conversation has always been a prize to me. Finding a person and picking them for all they're worth. You start with questions to see where they're going to end up. Especially in airports. If you can just get people to talk about themselves. That's what you do in a case study. I try to get someone's story.'

Graves also loves to act. When he teaches a graduate course in Foundations of Early Childhood Education, he spends part of each week impersonating the philosopher the class studies from Benjamin Franklin to Tolstoy to Piaget. Graves taught a course at the University of Vermont last summer for teachers called Understanding the Individual Writer. The writing process—the problem solving process that children, adults, and professional writers go through when they write—was the subject of the course. One student said, 'He literally showed us what kids do when they write. He sat there with one knee on the chair, his pencil in his fist, sounding out words. He even tore the paper with his pencil. He looked just like a little kid.'

When she went back to the classroom, she viewed her young authors with heightened appreciation and knew helpful ways to respond to them.

Graves watches and reflects on Chris and the other children. The research team compiles and analyses about twenty pages of data daily as they look for answers to questions and for questions they have not yet asked.

I asked Graves what he hoped to learn from this study.

'One, is to get a sense of sequences in which children learn to write, to see how much a child's development influences the writing process, to try to find out new components of the writing process, to come up with new questions. So little work has been done on the writing process. What does handwriting do for spelling and what do handwriting and spelling do for the writing process? And what does the writing process do for handwriting and spelling?

'This is not in the proposal—how can we help children and teachers in writing?'

'What are some things you've learned so far?' I asked.

Graves answered with a list of issues that would surprise an educational researcher, but not an anthropologist. Like an anthropologist who observes in the natural setting, Graves sees the tools of the first or third grade classroom as important. Tools are as much a part of the process as any other component. Writing is not done entirely in the author's head.

'Some things are little barriers. One, in the area of revision, just the mechanical problems involved in erasing a word. The labour —putting the writing on top of a black, smudged spot. You say, "Too bad they don't have materials that let them do that easily." Or with an older child, the dilemma of crossing out words or drawing arrows to another section to change the order or add new information. The child may think the teacher is the only person who can write on the paper. The dilemma of changing, scratching out. In time the child realises writing is clay and can be changed, and they do that. Children go into a plateau when they think the words are magic and unchangeable.'

Graves has observed children's impulses to change their original products. 'Art work, sequences of action. Both illustrations and writing deal with problems of space and time, how to represent them. How do you solve the problems of tools? Words are fixed in time and unchangeable. When children get dissatisfied, you can tell uneasiness. They are re-reading.

'I asked Carrie, a first grader, what would happen on the next page. First she said, "Wait and see." That was a cover-up. She didn't know. Then she said, "I don't know." Finally she said, "I guess I better think about it." She must think that's what you do when you don't know. I thought at the end of one page she was done. Then she started to draw furiously. I have a strong suspicion I threw her into rehearsing by asking those questions. A tree with a hole in it ended up, "The owl is home now."'

Carrie was working on a book of six pages of lined newsprint with unlined space at the top for drawing. It had a construction paper cover. 'This is an uneasiness I have about books too soon,' Graves said, relating tools to the writing process. 'Writing gets disjointed, writing just to fill up the book. When you turn the page, it's more difficult to relocate in time and space. It's a physical barrier the child has to overcome to go on to the next step, to get fluency. They have to be familiar enough with the process to change it. You don't get healthy unrest when something is brand new. When there's distance, there's something beyond what's mechanical and written at the moment.'

Months have passed since Chris wrote his menu for Snack Place, and Chris has overcome his reluctance to write anything longer or more complex than a menu. He wrote an eighteen-page book on *Star Wars*. Other titles include *Watership Down, Chemicals, The Moon, All About Aquariums, School,* and *The Sea.* Two have been published for the class library. Today he chose the best of his books and ranked the others. His criteria for good writing and his closely observed behaviour during the writing process will help other teachers see how to help their students develop as writers.

3. KDS CN RIT SUNR THN WE THINGK
Susan Sowers

'THER ARE DANGERUS CHEMICLES LIKE ASID,' Chris wrote in his book titled *ALL ABOUT CHEMICLES*. At the same table, Toni and Lisa worked on their writing, too. As Chris drew a chemist behind a lab bench, Kevin asked him how to install the periscope on his clay submarine. Other first grade children built robots with instrument panels in blocks, read books their classmates wrote and published, counted clusters of miniature frogs and recorded the sums in tiny equation books. Katy's mother helped three boys weave red and blue yarn into belts. Mary Ellen Giacobbe, a slender woman of thirty-two dressed in crisp slacks and a plaid shirt, dismissed the reading group. With deep-set grey eyes behind wire-rimmed glasses, she scanned the boys and girls at work and play among the low shelves and cabinets. 'You may go out for recess now,' she announced. A few children headed for the coat rack. Toni rescued her heroine from the green witch and waited, proud and smiling, to read her book to Giacobbe. When children had their choice of activities, someone always chose to write.

These children test as normal. Their scores span the range found in most classrooms. Yet they are gifted with the potential of six-year-old children. They are exceptional in their teacher: Mary Ellen Giacobbe. In her classroom at Atkinson Academy, the public school for Atkinson, New Hampshire, she has given children the tools they need to write.

Here is Kevin's fifteen-page, illustrated book, the first one he wrote, *All About Ants:*

Ains r mvn in a bld and ther wra insid and ot
A man kam to kal the adts and a lae was tik a baf
6 siks mnd kan to kal the adts ther r im tip fo the adts
Tje adts ther tid dkn the mi per siat bui
the adts r in the pis the man cot sime fo the adts
the adts cat a man
a man lqcd the adts
the adst r tak the gid
the mans mrn kid sim fo the adts
2 mant kid 1 nis and a mid adts
the mant fir a lich ovf the adts daf
a man kid 10 adst
the mant r win the mant sisitt fir on the adts
the adst r at hie the adst r in the kins

As Kevin read his story to Giacobbe, she recorded his words in correct spelling to help her remember his exact message. Then she typed his story in standard spelling and bound it in a book for the class library. Kevin read his published book before the class:

Ants are moving in a building. They are inside and outside.
A man came to kill the ants. A lady was taking a bath.
Six men came to kill the ants. They are on top of the ants.
The ants are tearing down the Empire State Building.
The ants are in the pipes. The men caught some of the ants.
The ants caught a man.
The man electrocuted the ants.
The ants are taking the gold.
The man's machines killed some of the ants.
Two men killed one nest and a mother ant.
The ants are losing.
The man threw a latch over the ants' door.
A man killed ten ants.
The men are winning. The men shoot fire on the ants.
The ants are at Hawaii. The ants are in containers.

'Kevin's humour and imagination and energy come through very clearly,' a critical adult would say. 'But what about all those errors and misspellings? Isn't the child being cheated by condoning errors and allowing bad habits to take root?'

'Spelling is a matter of habit for adults but not for children. They project this habit onto kids without bothering to investigate,' says Glenda Bissex. No one can accuse Bissex of not bothering to investigate. She is an educator and mother of a ten-year-old son, Paul. Paul learned to read and write through *invented spelling,* the name for this early kind of writing, without instruction. Bissex documented his growth in a case study for her doctoral dissertation for Harvard's Graduate School of Education. 'Invented spelling is really invented and new every time. When a word comes up again, it is invented again.'

Parents don't worry about errors when a child learns to talk, but they may worry about errors in writing too early. Bissex said, 'Errors are a piece of information rather than something to be erased.' They tell us as much about what children know as about what they don't know. Kenneth Goodman, a pioneer in the use of errors or 'miscues' to diagnose a child's strengths and weaknesses in reading, has called errors 'a window on the mind'.

Like children learning to talk, Giacobbe's children are trying to figure out the rules of written English. When Joshua wanted to write 'radio', he pronounced the word several times and wrote 'r d o'. 'There's another sound here,' he said pointing to the space between 'r' and 'd', 'but I'm not sure what.' He said 'radio' again and filled in the letter 'a'. Joshua explained, 'First you hear the beginning and end sounds. Then you hear the sounds in the middle.'

Kevin carried out the same kind of analysis on most of the 138 words he spelled in his story about the ants. Joshua described the sequence most beginning inventive spellers follow. First, they represent words with only one letter, the letter that stands for the first sound in the word. Kevin is more advanced. He hears the first and last sounds in most words. Although he remembers a few words from reading — 'the', 'a', and 'of' reversed to 'fo' — he relies on the sound of his speech. Kevin pronounces 'bath' as 'baf' and writes it as it sounds. He says 'lectrocuted' and writes 'lqct'. In 'Hawaii' (hie) and 'latch' (lich), Kevin hears the end of the words correctly. In 'building' (bld) and 'door' (daf), he does not. This is Kevin's second year in first grade, and he receives special help in reading and occupational therapy. Kevin will learn to hear and spell the sounds at the end and in the middle of words as he reads and writes every day.

Invented spelling gives young writers early power. Professional writers don't worry about correct spelling on the first draft and neither do inventive spellers. They work like writers who don't stop to look up a word in the dictionary. They need precise and lively words to tell their stories. Kevin wanted a container — not a can — to stop the ants. Giacobbe placed a list of seasonal words like 'sleigh' and 'reindeer' at the writing table before Christmas. 'But they ignored my list,' she said with a laugh.

Emily has a cowlick in her blond hair and gaps and new teeth in her smile. She is famous as the author of the Woody Owl books. Last fall as the days grew shorter and the nights longer, she wrote, 'I haitt naet I love moneg' (I hate night. I love morning.). Three days later she wrote a book about a frightening storm at night. She drew a little girl in bed. Tears covered the blanket and lightning flashed at the window. Emily blackened the room but left an open spot.

'That's my night light,' she told Lisa. 'My night light is very bright. It shines all over my bed. Besept a little dark is over it. I'm so frightened I don't feel like going to sleep.' Then she wrote, 'I haet naet it is bok I love morneg.' (I hate night. It is dark. I love morning.)

Two months later the days began to lengthen, and Emily wrote a book called, *The Prretty Lettle Girl:*

the prritty little gril	The pretty little girl.
her named is krisden	Her name is Kristen.
she love flawrs the bast	She loves flowers the best.
she haets school the wrst	She hates school the worst.

After Emily drew the little girl in her bedroom, a face with sharp teeth in its mouth appeared on the page. 'Now wait a doggone minute!' Emily said. 'A bad guy. He's come to kidnap her.' Then she wrote.

she jumpet up	She jumped up.
she was skaerd	She was scared.
she sow the vaillin	She saw the villain.

'Wait, the bulb fell out,' Emily said. She drew a globe on the floor. 'That's the night light falling down. He's sorry. She punched him out.' Emily finished her story:

she punched hem	She punched him.
shes so glad	She's so glad.
shes aslep	She's asleep.

Emily won a victory over her fear of darkness and celebrated in a book.

Giacobbe's students are exploring more than the conventions of language. She knows children do not need to blow bubbles or visit the zoo in order to have something to write about. She will never assign them to write 'I Am an Ice Cream Cone' or give them the first sentence of a Martian adventure. Children tap their own reserves of experience when they write as they do when they talk, draw, and play. They write as though entitled to this form of expression which their parents may fear.

In his study on the status of writing for the Ford Foundation, Donald H. Graves found most adults associate writing with the discipline of grammar and spelling. But published writers place these editing concerns at the end of the writing process when a piece is nearly finished and ready to be shown to a reader.

Six-year-olds must also explore their own interests without fear of violating the rules of writing etiquette. Sandy, an advanced student of arithmetic, wrote *The Book About Nine* to explain that number's special properties. She is also the author of a humorous book called *Spying on Mrs Giacobbe.* Jimmy is a small boy who writes about powerful racing cars, *Big Foot,* and a bionic hero, *Steve Austin.* Michael catalogued his new knowledge in *All About Dinosaurs.* Kevin maintains the moral order of the universe whether the good guys destroy the bad guys in outer space or in World War II. Diane celebrated Thanksgiving with a turkey dinner and brought the turkey to life again. Katy recalled a happy day of ice fishing with her family. Children explore the death of a pet or fear of the dark; they celebrate special days and friendships as well.

Giacobbe's children would not write as much or as well if she did not support them with publication and an audience. Emily read *The Pretty Little Girl* standing beside Giacobbe, their heads bent over the book. 'There's the night light, the door, the wall, a flower in her hand.' Emily read the next page, 'She loves flowers the best. She hates school the worst.'

'She hates school, Em?' Giacobbe asked with a direct look at her.

'Except on Thursdays. Then she has gym,' Emily said.

'Is the little girl you?' Giacobbe asked with a smile.

'It's just a dream. But she goes to school here. She's coming to this class, too.' Emily read the rest of her story.

'I like the way you introduced the girl here, and then told us what she likes — a little more about her — on the next page. And then you told us what she did, how she fought the villain. Finally she went back to sleep. Thank you for sharing your book with me.

'Remember, we were talking about periods?' Giacobbe asked.

'Oh, yeah,' Emily said. She reread her book and placed a period at the end of each sentence.

Emily placed her book on the table in the class library. Before lunch the twenty-one children meet on the rug, a colourful patchwork of carpet samples Giacobbe stitched together with fishing line. There they read, listen, and discuss the morning's books.

Later Giacobbe explained that Emily had an unhappy day at school yesterday. 'So I wasn't surprised when "the pretty little girl" hated school the worst. First I assigned Emmy some work in her math book. Then other work and special programs kept her from writing,' she said. A prolific writer, Emily was frustrated because she couldn't write.

'With the traditional worksheet approach to reading and writing, some kids would be so far ahead of her just because they can sit still and fill in the blanks. But not this way. It's scary to think what would have happened to her.'

Giacobbe's conferences with children rest on a more thorough knowledge of the child than red-pencilling worksheets can give her. 'I like to type their stories,' she said. 'It gives me a chance to think about that child.'

Giacobbe responds to the content of the child's writing. In previous months, Giacobbe tried to show Emily that her stories did not always make sense. When Emily protested that her Woody Owl book, published months ago, did not make sense, Giacobbe published a revised second edition. Today Chris will learn the difference between 'they're' and 'there', but Giacobbe first recognises his growing body of knowledge about chemistry. She will remind Toni that readers become confused when the words of her text travel from the bottom to the top of the page, but first she hears Toni's story. After Jimmy reads his racing drama, she will share Jimmy's pride that his father 'put smoke in the other guy's face'. Then she will work with him on hearing the 'f' sound since he spelled 'father' and 'face' with 'l'. Jimmy began to write with only twelve consonants and learned more as he needed them.

'R U DF' (Are you deaf?) Paul wrote at the age of five as though demanding to be heard. Paul wrote before he could read, without instruction. Glenda Bissex, his mother, has documented his growth as a writer and a reader in a five-year case study for her doctoral dissertation which was published by the Harvard University Press in 1980. Paul learned about reading and writing when he saw his mother writing in a notebook and when she read stories to him. Before he was five years old, he printed an array of letters on a banner to welcome his mother home. Not long after that, Paul tried to cheer her up when she was sick with a card full of scattered letters.

'How he learned to make letters and learned their names is a mystery. All this time, I knew nothing about invented spelling, even when he started,' said Bissex. On his own, Paul learned some basic principles of written English: we write from left to right and top to bottom of a page, and letters represent the sounds in words. After he wrote his first message, Paul discovered he could read what he had written. Others could, too, if his symbols matched what they expected a word to look like. Paul learned to read other authors' words before he went to school, but after he learned to read his own.

Maria Montessori, noted educator and Italy's first woman doctor, observed invented spelling seventy years ago. She was the director of Casa dei Bambini, a day care facility for children of Rome's factory workers. She noticed that preschool children who had been taught the alphabet but who could not read were composing words with letters.

Only a few educational researchers have investigated invented spelling. It is sometimes incorrectly thought to be found only among the children of professors and linguists. Perhaps because they are more knowledgeable about the development of language in children, they can identify their children's behaviour and tolerate the non-standard spellings. Montessori's young working class writers show that invented spelling is not limited to the children of well-educated parents.

The idea that writing can precede reading seems strange at first. Yet the first human ever to read a written symbol must have written it before reading.

Giacobbe's students are soaring above minimal competencies without the paraphernalia of management-by-objectives reading systems that require frequent rounds of testing, recording scores, and prescribed seatwork. I asked Giacobbe how she had started her students writing.

'When I came back from visiting another classroom where the children used invented spelling to write, I showed them the books the other children had made. They said, "That's cinchy. *We* can do that!" And they've been writing and reading their books ever since. They're not very interested in reading the books from the library yet. They're most interested in reading *their* books.'

Nearly one hundred books written and illustrated by the young authors lined the library shelves. Giacobbe keeps the first drafts in a file to help her evaluate their writing progress. To make each book, Giacobbe glues wall paper on cardboard covers then sews the pages to the backing tape with dental floss. Today was Jimmy's day to be librarian. He stamped the date on a card and put it in the pocket. He placed Lisa's newest book, *All About Going to the Movies,* in a plastic bag so she could take it home to read to her family without damaging it.

'Last year so much time was taken up with worksheets, there wasn't time to write. Every day they had tapes to listen to, a new art project, math, and reading worksheets. I had their time so occupied, they had no time to write. Children need to do the things they want to. Some may call it play. Once I read that play is a child's work. I believe it more and more.

'It really doesn't teach them to take responsibility for their learning if you tell them what to do every minute.'

'Mrs Giacobbe!' Craig interrupted. 'The gerbil — he's escaped! Chris, come help us!'

Readers and writers looked up and builders stood to catch a glimpse of Chippy running and slipping on the smooth floor.

'Craig, do you think you and Chris can find Chippy and put him back in his cage?' Giacobbe asked. They dropped to the floor and slid on the knees of their jeans to trap Chippy.

Giacobbe continued, 'Chris wanted to study dinosaurs, *right now.* And I thought, I have this beautiful unit on dinosaurs — books, posters, games, activities, everything. I've always used it after we come back from Christmas. But I thought, we always think *we* know when and how to teach them. But we don't! They know when it's time to do the things they need to do.

'And I really thought they had to be spoon fed — that I had to tell them what to write and when to write.

'They feel they can read anything because their writing is accepted. I was reading *James and the Giant Peach* to them. I made it a point to stop at a very exciting place. They wanted to know what would happen next. They said to me, "We can read the next chapter by ourselves." I've never had a class where they think everything's so easy.'

Michael and Steve waited at the round table where the children meet for reading instruction and writing conferences. They exchanged the books they had just written.

Gary, an ambitious young reader, sat alone at the end of the room reading *The Five Chinese Brothers.* 'He's writing the words he can't read,' Giacobbe explained. 'It's his idea.' As he wrote the unfamiliar words, he discovered he could read most of them and he erased the ones he could read.

'They know it's not just first and last letters or some random pattern of letters. They know what's involved because they've written.'

Glenda Bissex urged parents of a preschool inventive speller to answer their child's questions. 'There were things Paul just couldn't figure out for himself. Some things he asked for again and again until he got it right. He wanted to know and he got information when he asked for it — two pretty important conditions for learning. Children don't discover rules in a vacuum. Specific information *does* need to be supplied.

'There are different levels of tolerance for frustration among kids. Paul had enough confidence in himself to know he'd come out on the winning end. There's nothing wrong with frustration if it's challenging, only if it's defeating. Kids were frustrated learning to walk. Failure is not accepted in school. In that context, failure can be damaging.'

Fortunately, we're wise enough to let children fall down when they learn to walk. We don't punish a baby who falls or assign corrective exercises in balancing. Families quote their children's fearless early message and delight in the emerging person who wants to talk to them. Children can learn to write on their own before they read if we can help them develop their abilities.

'Learning to spell is a matter of knowledge, not habit,' said Bissex. 'Kids are trying to figure out the rules. Children are already abstracting at two years old. I have a sense learning starts globally. With babbling, kids speak globally rather than by words. They don't have a system building up from small units to bigger ones. A way to program a machine is not a way to teach a child.'

Toni writes letters to her father and puts them in his lunch box. Most first grade children fill in duplicated worksheets. Their teacher's red marks tell them whether they are right or wrong. When Toni's father comes home from work, his response to her letters will show Toni that writing is a powerful tool she can control.

The benefits of invented spelling have not yet been measured and statistically analysed, but they are evident in Giacobbe's classroom. Children learn to write and they learn to read. They are active, confident learners.

Sunny works and plays at a new book — *My Baby Kusin's Berthday Partee.* Her first page shows an aerial view of twelve smiling relatives around a table with triangular slices of cake on the plates set before them. She writes as deliberately as she draws, supplementing the words she knows by habit (*my, day, baby*) with inventions that let her tell her story. Logic and custom demand that beginners practise spelling and grammar before they write. But Sunny has learned to write by writing.

4. Writing Taps a New Energy Source: The Child

Lucy McCormick Calkins

'PETER, DON'T YOU WANT TO GO OUT FOR RECESS?' Mrs Currier asks. 'Not yet,' the nine year old answers. 'I'm writing about my salamander's stomach.'

Mrs Currier looks across the room to Susie who is singing softly to herself. Their eyes meet and Susie blushes. 'My writing is a song,' she says. 'I started it last night when I was outside and I had so many feelings they needed a song. Now I'm trying to fix up what I wrote.'

The fourth grade teacher watches as Peter and Susie pull back into their writing, then she opens the desk drawer and lays her own draft before her. The room is silent except for the scratch of pencils.

A bell brings twenty-three fourth graders swarming into the classroom; a flurry of mittens and hats. 'Writing time!' The word spreads quickly. As the children cluster around the box of writing folders, they talk about their writing.

'I'm going to fix up my radio piece.'

'Does anyone want to conference with me?'

'Oh, good! I'm on a new piece!'

'I need to go to the library for some more information.'

Soon the room settles into a workshop hum, and one can again hear the scratch of pencils. Dr Donald Graves, director of the Writing Process Lab at the University of New Hampshire, says, 'When children are senders of information as well as receivers of it, there is a new kind of energy, a new kind of involvement.'

That energy is contagious. Teachers and children catch the bug from each other. At Atkinson elementary school in rural New Hampshire, public school teachers at every grade level put writing at the centre of the curriculum. In their budgets, teachers are asking for more pencils, more paper. Requests for ditto paper and textbooks are way down.

'Writing's become the context for much of our day,' one teacher says. Like many teachers in the school, she teaches language through writing and uses writing in the content areas. Her children even write word problems in math. 'I give easily as much time to writing as I give to reading and math,' she says, 'because I think it's just as important.'

The principal, Mrs Jean Robbins, says, 'In giving priority to writing, we say to children, "I know you have something worth saying and that what you are saying can be the basis for your learning".'

When children write, they reach for the skills they need. Writing demands initiative. Writers do not receive learning. They make it. Teachers at Atkinson find writing makes children become experts on ancient Greek traditions, a broken radio, the stomach of a salamander. They become experts also on pronoun agreement, punctuation, and cursive penmanship. Children want their messages to be seen and heard. The urge to tell leads them to pursue the skills they need.

The results are clear. At Atkinson, first grade parents came to Open House in October saying, 'My first grader thinks she can read anything: signs, labels, books. She's reading to her little brother!' They ask what reading program has wrought such wonders. The teacher, Mrs Giacobbe, tells them: writing.

In the upper elementary grades, parents are saying, 'I've never seen my son so involved in school. When he moves on to the next grade, be sure he's in another writing classroom.'

When children are involved, they learn more. At Atkinson school, achievement scores on the Iowa Test of Basic Skills have risen twenty points during the past seven years. This year the third graders scored in the 98th percentile on this test, according to national norms.

'The key word is trust,' Mrs Robbins says. Teachers at Atkinson trust children to write their own textbooks. Children write—and then, step by step, they learn the skills and information which they need to write well. This interest in writing is nationwide.

The guest book at Atkinson attests to the widespread interest in writing. People have come to this little rural school from Australia, Canada, and England as well as from many parts of the United States. At Atkinson, they visit classrooms at every grade level, classrooms which range from open class to traditional teaching. Despite the different levels and teaching styles, the approach to writing in each room is based on shared premises.

The Writing Process

In first and fifth grade alike, children at Atkinson experience the professional writer's cycle of craft. Visitors to Atkinson will find that during the writing workshop at every grade level, some children will be *rehearsing* for writing, while others will be *drafting* or *revising* what they have written. Meanwhile the teacher moves around the room; observing, encouraging, extending. Teachers want all their children to cycle through the writing process, each at his or her own pace.

The Writing Process in First Grade

In first grade, rehearsal is an especially important part of the composing process because many six-year-olds are present-tense oriented and cannot plan a piece until they sit down with paper in front of them. Even then, if you ask a first grader, 'What are you going to write about?' many are apt to say, 'How should I know, I haven't drawed it yet.'

Often when children draw, their pictures lead them to new content. Sarah had already written:

> The pretty little girl. Her name is Kristin. She loves flowers the best. She hates school the worst.

Sarah drew a nice picture of the girl in her room. Into the picture she drew a face with sharp teeth. Sarah seemed startled. 'Now wait a doggone minute! A bad guy! He's coming to kidnap her!' And her writing took off, following her drawing.

First graders often rehearse throughout the process of writing. They write a line, and then they talk or draw about the next thing that will happen. The child cycles through rehearsal and drafting.

Revision, for first graders, mostly means adding on. The young child often writes for the egocentric play of it, with little attention to an audience's need for information. Annie writes, 'Jessie hid under the table,' (JCE HD NR TLB) and neglects to say who Jessie is. Later her classmates will listen to the story. 'Who's Jessie?' they'll ask. When the young writer explains that Jessie is a baby terrier, the class will say, 'Why don't you put that in?'

Missy writes about a girl who tries to catch the wicked witch. 'What happened?' 'Does the girl catch her?' Missy's friends want to know more.

But adding on is not so easy as one might expect. The young writer will probably look at his page, screw his face up, and say, 'There's no room! What should I do, erase this page and put it in, then erase all the other pages to move it all back?'

Children need to be encouraged to 'mess up' the page. Mrs Giacobbe says to seven year old Chris, 'Put your hand on your page where there is neither drawing nor writing.' Chris reluctantly puts his hand in the upper left corner, over the head of his dinosaur. 'OK, Chris, you can add the information there.' And so, Chris writes *why* the Brontosaurus stayed in groups. 'To pertikt the yung.'

Chris looks at his page, with most of the words neatly lined along the bottom of the page, and then the added phrase in the top corner of the page. 'That looks stupid,' he announces. 'How will they know to read up there?'

Mrs Giacobbe turns the question back to Chris. 'What can you do?' she asks.

So Chris adds a tiny arrow beside his lower sentence, pointing up.

'Do you think they'll see it?' his teacher asks.

With a deep sigh, Chris takes his pencil and makes a great big arrow which winds up the margin. His page begins to resemble the writer's working manuscript.

Now, seven months later, Chris says, 'Revisement is easy. Just take in, take out, move around. No problem. Then copy it over or get it published and it'll be neat in the end.'

It's easier for first graders to change what they've written when they write in books (construction paper covers, with lined paper inside) rather than on single sheets of paper. If all their sentences are on one page, only the first and last sentences are accessible. The rest are buried in the middle of the piece. In books, however, pages can be thrown away and added.

When six-year old John read his book *'My Trip to the Football Field'* to his first grade classmates, they were confused. 'Your book went hippity-hop from one thing to the next,' Sharon said. 'It's like you went to sleep and had a crazy dream.' Later, John uses the class staple remover, Jaws, to help him unstaple his book. He puts pages in the right order and staples the book together again. John's writing process is not unlike the process that professional writers experience.

Like professional writers, John does not worry about his spelling and mechanics until after he has thought about his content. He writes and rewrites his book based on information. Only then does he conference with his teacher on spelling.

John may have many mechanical mistakes in his story, but Mrs Giacobbe selects only a few to work on in each book. These skills are recorded in a writing journal so that both teacher and child have a record of what they have worked on together. 'I usually find that the day after I teach something, the child begins to use it,' Mrs Giacobbe says. 'But if the child forgets, we look over the journal together and then the child goes back to his writing and corrects it himself.' In this way, Mrs Giacobbe holds her first graders responsible for the skills they've been taught.

The Writing Process in the Upper Elementary Grades

Children in the upper elementary grades also cycle among rehearsal, drafting, and revision. Yet they experience the stages in the writing process differently because they are older.

'My third graders often plan for writing on the bus, at home, or at recess,' Mrs Howard says. 'In school, they don't need to plan so much as they need to see they have something worth writing about.' Mrs

Howard, like other teachers at Atkinson, insists that writers choose their own topics. These are her reasons:

1. Deciding what you have to say is probably the hardest and most important part of writing. We cannot take this responsibility away from the writer.
2. As children consider, select, and reconsider their topics, they experience the revision process. This is often the first and easiest form of revision.
3. When writers write what they know and care about, their writing is their own. They are driven to make it good—they supply the initiative and the motivation.

For a little while, children try to avoid choosing their own topics. They recall old story starters, they beg for assignments, they retell television programs. They do not think their interests and projects and lives are worth writing about.

Mrs Howard begins the year by asking her students to bring in things from home that they know and care about. Jeremy brings an ant farm. Jonathon brings a map from his trip. The children pair off and interview each other about the things they have brought. As a child shares the story behind her broken tennis racket, or the significance of a well-worn teddy bear, she finds that the details of her life are worth telling. And she also learns what she knows. She sees the surplus of information at her disposal, and can begin to make choices. 'What's the most important thing about Teddy?' 'Where should I start?'

Mrs Howard's room is soon full of her children's interests and lives. The clean tooth display is replaced by a baseball collection. The shelves become display cases for model airplanes, caterpillar cages, and a Dutch doll. Dr Donald Graves has said, 'You can tell a good writing classroom by the presence of children's interests and information in the room.'

As the year progresses, Mrs Howard finds other ways to help children choose topics to write about. She encourages them to talk with each other, to brainstorm for topics. Sometimes she may begin a writing workshop by asking everyone to share their topic—in hopes that the children will get ideas from each other.

Children learn the writing process through personal writing. Later they transfer it to other forms of writing. Now rehearsal involves library research, interviewing, note-taking. Atkinson teachers realise that whether children write about the discovery of penicillin or a new baby brother, rehearsal does not mean outlining. Writers do not plan their entire piece before writing it, for they know new connections will be made as they write, and new questions will emerge. They know their organisation will evolve through drafts and redrafts, through seeing their piece, through shaping it, through holding it in their hands. Rehearsal, therefore, is a time to toy with ideas, to gather information, to sense direction. Rehearsal is a time to become ready.

For some children, rehearsal is a way to avoid writing. They will conference, brainstorm, draw . . . but don't put pencil to paper. Mrs

Currier finds ways to get these children writing. Tammy begins each writing session with a conference. Alan charts his daily word count. Peter prides himself in a growing list of finished pieces.

Most of Mrs Currier's fourth graders, however, move easily between rehearsal and drafting. They know that during a writing workshop, there is no alternative but to write. That requirement—and the challenge and fun of making meaning on paper—is enough to keep them cycling through the writing process.

Just as the line between rehearsal and drafting is often unclear, so, too, the line between drafting and revision blurs. Writers revise throughout the writing process. Mrs Howard says, 'I used to think children should finish a draft, then bring the completed piece to a conference for help in revision.' Now she finds revision is easier when it comes early in the process.

Mrs Howard introduced her third graders to revision through topic choice. She asked them to list ten topics and then choose the one they liked the best. Revision begins as selection. Soon she was asking the children to write several beginnings to a piece and then choose the one they liked. Some children continued to use these strategies throughout the year, others invented their own revision strategies. A few never got hooked on revision at all.

Upper elementary teachers, like Mrs Giacobbe, encourage children to 'mess up' their pages. Some teachers model the process. They write on the blackboard, then ask the children for suggestions. Soon the passage is full of scratch-outs, arrows, and codes for inserts. In some classes, children write on every other line so they'll have room to add on. In another class, children are encouraged to put early drafts aside when they write, so that the revisions will be significant changes in focus, organisation and information rather than just refinements and corrections of the previous draft. Recently Mrs Currier displayed children's scratched-out, well-worked drafts on a bulletin board called, 'Make It Messy to Make It Clear.'

Teachers in the upper elementary grades, like Mrs Giacobbe, emphasise that editing is only a small—and final—part of revision. Teachers focus first on the content:

> What are you trying to say?
> Which is your strongest section? Can you build on it?
> What other information do we need to know?
> Why is this topic significant to you?
> Can you make it more real to your readers?

Only later do teachers and children look together at the mechanics and language. Depending on a child's ability to sustain work on a piece, 'later' may mean four drafts later, or it may mean a second look at the child's first draft. During these final conferences, teachers continue to give the responsibility to the writer. Rather than merely correcting the child's mistakes, teachers ask questions and teach skills.

In an editing conference, Mrs Howard may ask questions like these:

Are there any extra words which can be taken out?
Are the words precise and honest?
Are the verbs active and strong?
Does the piece sound right?
What about paragraphs?

'I try to teach them two or three things about mechanics with each piece,' Mrs Howard says. She shows Alison *Roget's Thesaurus*. She helps Greg with paragraphs. She gives Kenny a list of spelling words to study.

Mrs Howard suggests her third graders borrow her red pencil and correct their own papers. Some students use dictionaries to correct their spellings. Other, less able students, circle words they think are wrong and go to each other for corrections. By the time children come to an editing conference, they've already corrected much of the paper.

'On the cover of their writing folders, I jot down the skills we cover in conference,' Mrs Howard says. 'I expect them to *use* these skills next time they write.'

How Is It Done?

• TIME

At Atkinson, teachers know that writing process takes time—lots of time. They give *at least* two and a half hours a week to writing. 'I used to think an hour, four times a week, would be a great length of time,' Mrs Currier says. 'I thought my fourth graders would get restless. But there are so many different stages to writing, and when there is time for sustained work, the stages all flow together.'

'The time for writing has to come from somewhere else in the curriculum,' Dr Graves points out. 'In American education, there's too much addition and not enough subtraction. Curriculums have become inflated.'

Atkinson teachers take time from other subjects and give it to writing because they know writing offers a context for learning these other skills. 'Writing has changed the whole curriculum,' Mrs Howard says. 'Last year I divided language into little parts—punctuation, spelling, reading, letter writing. I made up class lessons for everything and spent my time trying to convince the children workbooks were important.' Now Mrs Howard teaches these skills during writing conferences.

A study funded by the National Institute of Education shows that Mrs Howard's children are learning them more effectively than if they were doing drills, workbook exercises and language lessons. Researcher Lucy McCormick Calkins found that although Mrs Howard's third graders have no formal instruction in punctuation, they can define/explain an average of twice as many kinds of punctuation as can children in a third grade across the hall where writing is rare but punctuation is taught through daily classwork and drills.

• PACE

Writing is a laboratory subject. Like biology, drama and art, writing takes long blocks of time. Graves says, 'Life comes at us in memos and pieces. Writing process requires a pace which is qualitatively different. There must be time for careful listening to the evolving piece, time for responsiveness, time for sustainment.'

It is not enough to haphazardly find a few hours in most weeks to use for writing. When writing time is always changing, always stolen, children write as if there is no tomorrow. Nine year old Andrea says, 'I need to have all the time I want to work on a piece. If a teacher says, 'You have to get this done in a week,' then you write fast and you don't want to see mistakes and problems. You're afraid to find that it's not good, not what you wanted.'

When children rely on writing every Monday, they will rehearse for writing during the weekend. When they know they'll write again on Wednesday and Friday, they can dare to experiment and to look back. The pace is their own. They know there will be time to find their problems, to hound out their difficulties. They write with a spirit of exploration because the pace allows them to follow their language and their images towards new meanings.

• SCHEDULE

Most teachers have the same basic routine for writing time, day after day. 'I don't have to keep it varied, to dance on the table, as it were, to keep them interested. Writing is inherently interesting, as long as children write from their lives,' one teacher says. The writing teachers rarely begin their sessions with gimmicks to motivate. 'We don't need them,' they say. Instead, writing usually begins with children getting their writing folders, re-reading what they have already done, and getting to work.

For one fourth grade class, writing time extends out of a brief independent reading session. The children know to come in from recess and immediately get out their reading books. The room settles down. As children read, Mrs Currier moves amongst them, checking on their plans for writing that day. After fifteen minutes, the children begin their writing. And they have each had a brief writing conference already.

A class of fifth graders often begin writing workshop by spending ten minutes writing in a journal. Their teacher writes too, and then after a little while she encourages them to share their journals or to use them as rehearsal for their writing.

Mrs Howard usually begins writing by passing out folders. 'During writing workshop, children mostly write, and conference with each other and with me,' she says. 'Often at the end of the day we have a brief share meeting to talk about a few students' work-in-progress.'

• GROUP INSTRUCTION

Most of the teachers at Atkinson spend very little time on whole-class writing instruction. 'I do most of my class instruction during the share meeting at the end of the day,' Mrs Howard says, 'where I model responses to evolving drafts. Sometimes I also have a five or ten minute activity at the beginning of a workshop.' These are examples of the activities she might do with her class:

1. She passes out little bits of note paper to the children and asks them to each list 5 problems which writers often have (not enough detail, too big a subject . . .) and then to star the problem which they seem to be having. She asks each child to keep in mind the starred problem while rereading the draft.

2. The children gather in a circle and each tells where he or she is in the drafting process and what is the main idea. This is a chance for Mrs Howard to touch base with each child, and for children to realise their classmates are all into the same process. It also helps children to have to define their main idea.

3. Children are asked to pair off and read their evolving drafts to their partner. The listeners are asked to ask questions like, 'What's your favourite part?' 'What problems are you having?' 'Do you need any help?'

4. Mrs Howard chooses a child's first and final draft, and reads them out loud to the class to illustrate how revision helps to improve a draft. The children tell why the final draft is better. They discuss qualities of good writing.

5. Mrs Howard reads the beginning lines of published books in the class library, and they talk about how writers spend a lot of time working on their leads. Children go back and rewrite their leads four different times and then choose the one they like best.

6. Mrs Howard may use this time for management. 'Bring your writing folders to the meeting area,' she may say. 'Now check your Work-in-Progress folder. Does it have only the drafts of your present piece in it? Check your cumulative folder. Are all the drafts of each piece here, stapled in order onto the final draft?'

7. Mrs Howard may use this time to model writing, or to model good conferences, or to model 'messing up' the page.

- CONFERENCES

The writing teacher has been likened to the circus stunt man who sets plates spinning on the end of long sticks and then watches and when a plate begins to wobble, he moves over and with his finger-tip gives it more spin, and then watches again for when he is needed.

A writing conference may be merely a finger-tip on the shoulder, or an encouraging word. Or a writing conference may be a fifteen minute group discussion about a shared problem. In writing conference, Amy explains how to start a Go-Kart. Peter adds quotation marks into his piece. Sarah explains the significance of her topic. There is no set way to do writing conference.

Yet teachers agree on a few principles. Above all, they agree that the conference method of teaching writing gives responsibility to the writer. During conference, the teacher listens. She may listen to the *piece,* and respond to the subject. 'I'm glad you shared that with me, Becky. I never knew about that accident. How did you feel?' 'Peter, I can just picture those eyes in the night. They make me shudder. I can't wait to hear more.'

During conference, the teacher may listen not to the piece, but to the *process.* 'What problems are you having?' 'Have you read it out loud to yourself?' 'What do you plan to do next?'

Mrs Giacobbe asks these questions to her first graders. The Pulitzer Prize winning author of *A Writer Teaches Writing,* Donald M. Murray, asks these questions of his advanced journalism students.

Through questions, teachers extend the writer's process of weighing options, of making deliberate choices, of experimenting. Sometimes the piece gets better. Sometimes the piece gets worse. Teachers remember that the conference is not the time to teach qualities of good writing. These can be taught at the beginning of the workshop during five minutes of classwork. But the conference is a time to support and nurture the process. In the long run, the quality of writing improves alongside the process.

- OWNERSHIP

The different pace of writing leads to a different sense of ownership. 'I used to try to short cut things by assigning topics and correcting papers,' an Atkinson teacher says. 'But now I find when children choose their own topics and revise their papers based on their own decisions, they care about their writing. It belongs to them.' Ownership is worth the time it takes.

When children control the writing process, the teacher's role changes. Whereas once teacher's energy went into making up enticing topics, deciding how many drafts a piece needs, finding the problems in a draft, and making editing corrections, now these responsibilities belong to the child.

'Children become invested in their work. It is theirs. They want to do the best they can do,' one teacher says. When children have ownership of their piece, they supply the motivation, the energy. Teachers can observe, question and extend. Teachers, as well as children, experience a different pace, and with it, a different quality.

5. What Children Show Us About Revision
Donald H. Graves

SARAH STOPS, and with furrowed brow, looks again at the word, *jul* (jewel), she has just written, erases it, and over the same thin, blackened spot of lined newsprint paper she sounds and rewrites, *juwul.* Sarah sensed that something was missing when she first wrote. Sounding it through again confirmed that a *w* was needed. Six year old Sarah has been writing for a week; this is her first act of revision.

'Oops, I goofed. I don't want that,' says Brian. Brian, an eight year old, writes a story about a rescue. He erases *came to* and writes in *reached* for the sentence, 'Jay's father *reached* out to save me and pulled me up.' The meaning didn't fit; a new word was needed. Most of the changes Brian makes are still in the spelling adjustment category and are made when he first composes. He has just begun to change words because he wants more precise meaning.

Eight year old Andrea drafts and redrafts. First drafts are easily identified in her writing folder because the writing is large and hastily written. Jagged lines are drawn through whole sentences and parts of others, later to be recombined into new organisations in the second draft. Arrows are drawn from the bottom of the page to the top. New words are written in, others crossed out. There are no erasures. Andrew knows that drafts are temporary and lead only to more drafts.

55

Sarah, Brian and Andrea are three of sixteen children involved in an NIE funded study to document how—and in what order—primary children change composing, spelling, and motor behaviours *during* the writing process. This research, done in an elementary school in New Hampshire, will identify, describe, and sequence the order in which behaviours related to the writing process emerge over a two year period. This is the second* in a series of articles reporting data as they unfold in the study. This issue is devoted to early data and speculation on revision, as well as the implication of these data for the teaching of writing.

When Sarah, Brian and Andrea revise they show us what is important to them in the writing process. Sarah may be changing her paper because her teacher feels spelling is important. Nevertheless, it is at least a demonstration of what standard Sarah has adopted at the moment. Brian's change of *reached* for *came to* is concrete evidence of an intelligent unrest with words and ideas. When Andrea draws arrows and crosses out words after stating, 'How am I going to change this?', there is visible evidence of what problems confront her and how she solves them.

In this study, revision refers to the act of changing something already composed. It may be as simple as adjusting the shape of the letter *s* written seconds before or as complex as removing a second paragraph of an article and rewriting a fifth to move up to replace the second.

Sarah

Six year old Sarah revised before she began to write. Sarah adjusted blocks in her make-believe house to fit the need for an enlarged bedroom. Wings were sketched in on birds drawn the day before. Yarn was pulled out of a burlap pattern to start again because it did not follow the path she wanted. The tool of revision was part of her learning style; it merely continued when she began to write.

Although Sarah is just beginning to write, within two weeks she demonstrates behaviours that will serve her well in future writing. She rereads, adds words, proofreads earlier in her selection—all traits or tools that will be useful later on. They are traits that account for her rapid advancement as a writer. Sarah experiments, regresses, experiments, yet moves in the upward spiral where her script gains precision, and words more closely resemble exact spellings.

Unlike most beginning writers, Sarah did not rehearse through drawing or other practice constructions. Rather, she wrote in an impressionistic style, putting down spelling inventions and 'feels' of messages. If Sarah was asked, 'What will you write next?', she responded, 'I don't know.' Early in November Sarah wrote:

I waꙄ love Able ANd I waꙄ nieꙄ I loved her

Ꙅhe wꙄ aꙄ neiꙅ I loved her

---

*See *Language Arts* (NCTE), January 1979.

When Sarah added fourteen words to another story after she had finished writing, the words were feeling type words, *I love you, beautiful, pretty, nice.* Other children frequently said to Sarah, 'We don't get this.' Sarah merely shrugged her shoulders and said, 'That's the way I do it.'

On November 30th Sarah showed signs of changing. For the first time Sarah shared an advanced impression of what would be in her writing. She stated, 'And on this page I will say, and this one . . .' The new step, however, affected Sarah's writing when she wrote:

Woody is cot.	(Woody is cute.)
He tok a wrom.	(He took a worm.)
Woody did.	(Woody died.)
Woody wak.	(Woody wake.)
Woody good.	(Woody good.)
Woody neis.	(Woody nice.)

Unlike other writing episodes Sarah could not sit still during the composing of this simple message. For each two to four word sentences, she left her seat at least twice to visit other parts of the room. The message is unusual for Sarah because for the first time it has space-time boundaries and follows a pre-stated sequence. Whereas feeling sentences in other writing were dashed down in six to seven word units at six per minute, now the units are shorter and at three words per minute. Sarah did not do *any revision* during this new approach to writing. Getting the message down was enough; such behaviours as rereading, proofing or revising were not present.

The next day, December 21, Sarah's message had more coherence, and followed a more typical story-line. She did not move about or display the tension behaviours of the day before. Sarah wrote:

Ragebee Ann Ragedee Anndy

Oenc a poen a tame	(Once upon a time.)
Tare was soem dolls	(There was some dolls.)
Taer naems aer Ann	(Their names are Ann
and Anndy	and Andy.)
The valin is faetig	(The villain is fighting
on Ann from hrteg	on Ann from hunting
cuz Ann is a gial.	because Ann is a girl.)
Ha ha ha ha Ann is cot	('Ha, ha, ha, ha Ann is cute.'
she is said Anndy.	'She is,' said Andy.)
Taer aer good said the	('They are good,' said the
valin.	villain.)

Several changes are noted from the day before: sentences are more developed, *Once upon a time* makes its appearance, rereadings and revisions increase, and the logical construction *because* is introduced. The use of the word *because,* an attempt to explain central action, leads to a sentence with the 'sound' of logic but a confused meaning.

Other children liked the story but could not understand her sentence, 'The villain is fighting on Ann from hunting because Ann is a girl.' And Sarah could not respond to their queries. Again, the new step will not be revised in this stage of Sarah's development.

Most revision is at the word unit level, and involves the adjustments of spellings. Words go through stages of development along with the child. The stage of development for each, the child and the word, determines if there will be a revision. For Sarah and other children who invent spellings, words are written and revised in the following categories:

1. *Sight words:* These words have reached the stage of final, correct spelling. For Sarah such words as *good, she, is, said,* and *from* are in this category. The words are known, stable and will be revised if she spots an error in them.

2. *Stable inventions:* These words are spelled the same way each time even though they are inventions. Such words as *valin—villain, neis—nice.* Since these words have reached a point of stability, differences in them will be noted and revised.

3. *Words in transition:* These words are invented, have appeared only several times in the child's writing. When these words appear, the child sounds them through as they are written. An example of this type of word for Sarah is *wuz, wsas* in her earlier writing. The word is now in the sight category. Words in this category are not revised as often as sight words and stable inventions since they are unstable.

4. *First inventions:* These are new words invented for the first time as in *botafll prnssas—beautiful princess.* Of all words spelled, these are the least likely to be revised. If these words are revised at all it is during the composing of the word itself.

In summary, Sarah's revision patterns are shaped by a variety of circumstances. Word stability, the newness of a procedure, audience response, the purpose of the writing, are all factors affecting Sarah's revising habits. It is the intent of this study to observe these same factors in the writing processes of the other sixteen children.

Brian

From September through November eight year old Brian wrote easily. He composed at an average speed of five words per minute. Misspelled words produced a mild dissatisfaction. Like many other children his age, the major motor and spelling problems were overcome in the first two grades.

Most of Brian's writing was fiction—racing cars, a circus, a rescue. Two were stories about his father and grandfather. All five, however, followed a retelling of a story already rehearsed by Brian when he told it to family members or classmates. For this reason, Brian had a strong, advanced concept of what happened next. Such queries as, 'Tell me what will happen next' or 'What will this be about?' brought two to three paragraph responses. When Brian wrote, he seemed to fill in the blanks of his advance story concept. The actual writing followed pre-stated paragraphs closely. If Brian did revise, it involved spelling adjustments when he first composed the word.

During the last week of November, Brian changed the way he wrote and revised. Brian's teacher was responsible for the change.

Noting Brian's level of fluency, yet lack of revision, she stressed two new approaches to the writing process. One required Brian to write about a personal experience, the other to write three leads before beginning to write the main paper.

Brian's teacher believed that revision is easiest when it relates to writing about personal experience. It is easier to confirm the truth of personal experience than the stories of fantasies. 'That was the way I felt; no, I didn't feel that way; it must have been this way.'

Brian's teacher aided the concept of revision at two different points in the prewriting. Brian wrestled through a listing of four different experiences before deciding on the one he wished to write about. The inclusion and exclusion of topics is a process of revision. 'This is suitable; that is not suitable.'

Three leads were written to start his personal account of losing his breath in the second grade. Brian wrote:

> I have a problem with my ribs. If I get hurt bad on my left side I can't breathe!
> Once when I was in second grade, I was on the see-saw and I fell off! I can't breathe!
> I couldn't talk! I was trying to say I can't breathe!

Unlike other children who had not grasped the concept of multiple starts, Brian's second and third leads were not the second and third sentences of a three sentence story. Each lead was a partial revision of the other. Each had the phrase, 'I can't breathe,' with different beginnings. With each draft the language becomes more direct until Brian simply writes, 'I couldn't talk!'

A week later Brian wrote three leads for another personal experience. In the midst of the second lead, he said, 'Oh, no, this isn't what I want'—he smiled, and crossed out the unwanted phrase. Up to this time Brian erased all errors.

Once crossing-out enters the picture for Brian or other children, the units of revision expand. To erase an entire line or even a phrase is a large task and usually quite messy. The draft now takes on an important, temporary quality. Words can be written in; others excluded. The section may be written from three to four times before the words are true to the meaning of the personal experience. Furthermore, the child realises print is not indelible, does not have to be correct the first time, is a means toward a more permanent end.

Once children like Brian feel their control of the writing process from the choice of the topic and selecting the best lead to the clarification of experience through several drafts, a Copernican revolution has taken place. The centre of control is more in the child's hands than the teacher's. Output doubles, revision increases ten-fold, sentences are crossed out, paragraphs rearranged. Word unit revision is practised only as a touch-up process in the final draft.

In this case study of children's writing it is sometimes difficult to know where development ends and instruction begins. The dilemma is not unlike the heredity-environment issue. Environment activates the genetic potential, just as the teaching environment interacts with the child to activate development. We still maintain our belief that a teacher cannot draw upon non-existent schemas but can lead the child to juxtapose already existing schemas to produce a third. A child with an experience, the words to recall it, and the reading power to disengage from his own written text, can be led to revise.

Andrea

In September eight year old Andrea wrote at a speed of 15.5 words per minute, an unusually high speed for children her age. The handwriting was legible with most words spelled correctly, the familiar plateau reached by Brian and children who have mastered the motor and sound-symbol components of writing. The stage is not unlike that reached by readers who are proficient decoders yet who need to use reading as a tool for personal development.

Andrea wrote as many as 500 words in a sitting but did not revise. In September she did minor revising through the 'proofing' of words *as* she wrote. She revised as she wrote since only one writing draft was involved. The revisions were low level—change in letter shapes, a missing vowel to make a correct spelling.

Andrea's first content revision came on October 2nd when reading for spelling errors in her selection. She noticed a problem in the logical outcome of an incident. She reached for her pen but hesitated, not knowing how to adjust the problem.

Andrea's dilemma of how to revise once she knew a revision was necessary raised many questions that must be observed as part of this study. Andrea might have asked:

1. If this first draft is due how can I make this change and not have to do the entire paper over?
2. Where do I write the change in; all the words are close together and the lines are too?
3. Isn't the teacher the only one to make changes on the paper?
4. If I did pass the paper in with the change wouldn't it look messy?

Visibly Andrea was concerned with space and aesthetic issues, 'How can I fit it in and make it look neat?'

Up until the middle of October all of Andrea's writings were imaginary stories. Her final story in the genre was on an assigned Halloween topic. Andrea started by drawing; as the drawing evolved she stated, 'I know more what it is going to be about. Ghosts go to meetings and plan how to scare people.' But Andrea drew since she has little opportunity for rehearsal. Andrew wrote an imaginative, adequate story but when it was completed the researcher asked, 'If you were to improve the story, what would you do?' Andrea did not know how she could improve the story.

Andrea had the potential to revise but did not. She had already expressed an interest in adjusting a logical problem in content. Her stories were well-developed with good characters and complex sequences of action. Furthermore, she was a good critical reader of other writings. Still, Andrea's development as a writer had reached a plateau. On October 12 Andrea's teacher provided the appointment to release her potential as an effective, revising writer.

Like Brian's teacher, Andrea's asked the children to write about a personal topic, something that had happened to them. Prewriting was aided when children interviewed each other about their experiences, and then practised leads before writing. It is important to note that each of these emphases carries its own built-in opportunities for revision.

1. Choose a topic, a topic that has happened to you.

Andrea thought, and recalled an incident when she tried to fly.

2. Ask a friend to interview you about your topic.

The interview began with a discussion of a bird nest and ended up with Andrea telling about an incident when she tried to fly with some wings her father had made.

3. Don't start to write until you have tried three leads.

Andrea wrote three leads with each lead an improvement over the one before.

(Note that each is a *revision* of the other, not a new incident.)

Andrea wrote:

Lead 1: Once when I was very little I got a hank to fly, so I tried jumping off things and tried to float up and across.

Lead 2: I always wanted to fly, but whenever I tried it, I always fell Kaboom on the ground.

Lead 3: Kaboom! That hurt! Why can't I fly? The birds do. Even with these wings, nothing happened.

Each lead was more immediate. Furthermore, Andrea knew it since she chose the third as her best because, 'It's happening now.'

Andrea's handwriting changed during the writing of the three leads. Whereas before the writing was smaller, neater and erased when errors were made, now the writing is in a large scrawl suggesting the temporary nature of draft writing. Note how this view changed when Andrea wrote her first lead. By the start of the second sentence, Andrea knew the writing was temporary.

Learning to fly

Once when I was very little I got a hank to fly So I tryed jumping of things and tryed to float up and across I tryed and tryed til my father made me and my sister big card board butterfly wings.

Now it is December and Andrea revises her 500-700 word papers three to five times each. Her revisions involve such advanced characteristics as: paragraph deletions; reordering sentences and paragraphs; insertions of new information. She continually reads drafts to child and teacher audiences, listens, and revises again. Andrea is even more advanced than Brian in the length of time a selection will evolve. Whereas Brian's selection evolves over a week's time, Andrea will maintain her revision and interest over a three-week period. As long as children continue to control the information and sense the continued improvement of the paper, the writing carries on. For some eight-year-old children, one to two days is the present limit, for others like Andrea, three weeks.

Summary of Preliminary Findings on Revision

Early data already show some trends useful to the teacher of writing. Although only three cases are reported here in this article on revision, data from other children play a part in adding weight to these early findings. Some of these trends may change, yet other professionals will find it useful to test these early findings for themselves. The research team would welcome an exchange of views with others who have observed children's practices in writing.

1. Children revise in other media forms such as block building, drawing and painting before they revise in writing. Children who demonstrate an overall learning stance toward revision in one area are more likely to demonstrate it in another such as writing.

2. When children try a new approach to writing, other areas in which they have been competent may suffer temporarily.

3. Beginning writers do not revise. Getting the new step down is enough. (When Sarah introduced a logical construction, she did not revise it even though it did not make sense to her.)

4. Early writing is often impressionistic. Children put words down for a certain feeling. Feelings are revised only if the child senses the feeling is not accurate. (Sarah 'sprinkles' in 'It is good', 'I love you' after her work is completed.)

5. Invented spellings go through stages of development along with the child. They fall into different classifications—first inventions, words in transition, stable inventions, sight words. Words that are more stable, as in stable inventions and sight words, are more likely to be revised.

6. Toward the end of the primary years many children reach a point of equilibrium when handwriting and spelling problems are behind them and messages flow easily on to the paper. Children do not revise these messages.

7. Eight-year-old children find it easier to revise topics about personal experiences than the experiences of others. They find it easier to recall their own experiences than the experiences of others.

8. Revision begins when children choose their own topics. Children who quickly arrive at a number of topics, learn to exclude some topics and write on others, are learning to revise.

9. Children who can quickly list personal topics for writing, and write a series of leads about the same subject, demonstrate a strong capacity for revision.

10. Peer audiences have an effect on children's revision and their use of new approaches to the writing process.

11. Teachers can play a significant role in releasing a child's potential for revision. (Note procedures used by Brian's and Andrea's teachers.)

12. When children no longer erase, but cross out, draw lines and arrows for new information arrangements, or change their handwriting to a scrawl, they indicate a changed view toward words. Words, for these children are now temporary, malleable, or clay-like. The words can be changed until they evolve toward the right meaning for these children.

13. Children who write rapidly are more likely to revise in larger units and sustain a single composition for a longer period of time than those who write slowly. (Andrea writes at 15 words per minute, does three or four drafts over a three week period, whereas Brian writes at 5-6 words per minute, does two drafts over a one week period.)

6. Children Learn the Writer's Craft
Lucy McCormick Calkins

'LOOK OUT!' the six-year-old cried. 'The enemy is comin'.' Alex pencilled a wobbly spaceship onto the corner of his paper. 'Boom! Boom! Pkeeeoow!' The first grader beside Alex glanced up in time to see giant swirls of pencil flames spread over Alex's paper. Soon Alex had destroyed his careful spaceships. Only a scribble remained.

Now Alex writes, 'The whole world was destroyed.'

THE HL WD WZ DSD

He mutters to himself, 'Destroyed. Deeeee-stroyed. E. I hear an E.' With his thick red pencil, Alex piles a dark E on top of the letters DSD. 'Destroyed.' Again he sounds the word. 'Deee-stroy-ttt.' A *T* is added on top of Alex's already illegible smudge of letters. 'There, I spelled that one good, I did,' Alex announced proudly to himself.

Alex doesn't care that his marks are illegible. He rarely looks back to notice how letters look, and he never volunteers to show his finished papers to a reader. Alex writes, spells, and represents for the sheer fun of it. There is no goal beyond the doing. Process is everything. Writing, for Alex, is play.

When nine-year-old Amy writes, she shifts between fast, impulsive composing and close, careful tinkering. For a few minutes she may spill bold print onto the page, writing at the unusual rate of twenty words a minute. 'All of a sudden I think of an idea and I'm writing wicked fast,' the nine-year-old said after one such spurt. Then her hand stops. Amy pulls into the draft and views it with the critical eye of a reader.

'I like this part,' Amy may say as she traces around one section of the paper. She begins a second draft, a third. Some drafts spill themselves onto the paper. Others are carefully crafted. As Amy writes, she cycles between playful involvement with the process and critical concern with the product. This is the writer's cycle of craft.

This paper is the story of writing as it shifts from play to craft. It is the story of Amy and of Alex, and also of fourteen other children. Through a grant from the National Institute of Education, Donald Graves, Susan Sowers and I are observing these children in their classrooms. We will follow them on a day-to-day basis for two years. We selected the eight first graders and eight third graders because they represent a wide span of developmental levels. Alex is one of the lowest children in our developmental scale. At the opposite end of the spectrum is nine-year-old Amy.

Through video-tapes, observation notes, and xerox copies of their work, we are documenting and studying their development as writers. We are building a tentative developmental map of how children change composing, penmanship and spelling behaviours during the writing process. This paper will follow changes in children's writing process in order to illustrate how their writing moves from play to craft.

In his book, *The Arts and Human Development,* Howard Gardner writes:

> The play impulse becomes the art impulse (supposing it is strong enough to survive the play years) when . . . it becomes conscious of itself as a power of shaping semblances which shall give value for other eyes or ears and shall bring recognition and reknowing. [Wiley NY 1973, p. 166]

When Alex piles letters into a smudge and explodes drawings into a scrawl, he is not 'shaping semblances which shall give value for other eyes or ears . . .' The six-year-old cannot envision an eventual audience or regard his work as a product. He can't shift into an imagined future. He can't climb out of his own shoes and become a reader. He can't view his piece through the eyes of another person.

Amy shifts between involvement and distance, between writer and reader. Her perspective on a draft is flexible and controlled. Her time and space framework encompasses both the play-like, all-present, all-personal quality of Alex's writing and the conscious 'shaping of semblances . . . for other eyes or ears . . .' which Gardner suggests is one distinguishing quality of art.

This is the story of the stages and sequences between Alex and Amy, between play and craft.

Writing as Play

Alex sweats when he writes. Sometimes he spends several minutes toiling over a single word. His fingers cramp from squeezing the fat red pencil. Writing is hard work.

The playfulness of Alex's writing comes not because it is easy but because the time and space dimensions of his writing are like those of play. There is no planning, and there is no goal. For Alex, writing, like play, is present-tense.

When it is time to write, six-year-old Alex picks up his pencil and begins. There is no delay. If a researcher asks, 'What will your story be about?' Alex is dumbfounded by the stupidity of the question. 'How should I know,' he says. 'I haven't written it yet.' Then Alex begins to write. He prints whatever comes to mind, to pencil point. He doesn't deliberate over topic-choice or the lay-out of his drawing and words. In his egocentricity, Alex does not—indeed, he cannot—get outside himself and consider what topics his readers might enjoy.

The people in the story all die and have funerals. Alex shoves the paper into his cubby and immediately joins the highway crew in the block area. Writing ends as abruptly and as completely as it began.

During the early part of first grade, Sarah, like Alex, was oblivious to the needs of an audience. She chose her topics easily, and was content to play with the sounds and textures of language when she wrote. Writing was messing about in her medium.

All About Yellow
Yellow is stronger than blue and red. I love purple instead. Orange sits on hat. Yellow sits on cat. Red sits on mat to cat to hat. Yellow is nice. I love yellow best. I love purple. Red and yellow fight. They won't stop until they are done. Yellow is a piece of sun. They have fun so yellow is the best.

Other children would listen to Sarah's stories and say, 'Your book is silly, Sarah,' or 'I don't get it.' Sarah didn't care. She wrote for herself. Researcher Susan Sowers comments, 'Sarah (was) still too egocentric to let her audience spoil her play.' [*Language Arts* NCTE October 1979]

By February, Sarah's audience was beginning to spoil her play. She wrote less. Unfinished books accumulated in her folder. Nothing satisfied her anymore. Her increasing sense of audience deadlocked her into writer's block.

Sarah's classmate, Annie, also does not consider a future audience in early first grade. Annie reads, 'We kept on losing Hilary.'

WEN KAPTON LOSING HELARE

As she turns the page, Annie explains her meaning to the children around her. 'Hilary is only one year old so that's why we kept on losing her. We lost her under the tablecloth.'

Annie knows this information is important, yet she doesn't put it into her book. She considers only her present audience, the people who are alongside her during the writing process. She doesn't distance into the future and imagine her writing as a product or her readers as separate from herself.

Annie's classmates will hear her story and ask, 'Who's Hilary?' Annie will explain her writing, and later, as she sits at the round conference table with her teacher, Annie will be encouraged to add information into her story.

Before long Annie will consider the needs of an audience while she's writing. Her classmate, Laura, has begun to internalise her audience. While Laura writes she holds an internal dialogue with an audience. She writes,

MY FAMLY LIKES PEANUT BATTR

Laura knows the other children will say, 'Why do they like peanut butter? You have to tell us why,' and so Laura mutters to herself, 'I already told you why.' When Laura writes

AND I PLAYED A GAME

she says, 'Oh-oh, they're going to kill me,' and erases *game*. She writes the specific game, 'Aggravation'.

AGOUSHON

Few professional writers share Laura's constant audience awareness. Most writers need time to write for the play of it. Hopefully Laura will re-learn to write for herself as well as for readers. John Ciardi describes the writer's craft by saying:

> 'The last act . . . of writing must be to become one's own reader. It is, I suppose, a schizophrenic process. To begin passionately and to end critically, to begin hot and to end cold; and, more important, to try to be passion-hot and critic-cold at the same time.'

Writing Becomes Less Playful

The onset of conventions is often an early indication that children regard their writing as an entity which exists after the writing process is finished.

Young children put emphasis into their writing for the play of it rather than for the sake of communication. They may darken important words or put them in capitals. A young child darkens the *pull* of a fishing line. The emphasis is not for an audience, nor is it deliberate. The memory is exciting and so the child's arm moves in big strokes.

Later, this child may ask, 'What punctuation do I use to make them read this loud?' Punctuation can tell a distant audience how to read a passage, when to pause, where to raise their voices, which words to emphasise. When children begin to view writing as product as well as process, they will differentiate the immediate expressive quality of speech and the more autonomous, distanced mode of written text. Children will want writing to communicate to a distant audience. This may lead to a new concern for conventions and correctness.

The child's emerging concern with 'the correct way' shows development toward a broader time frame. Peter spells a word and then rereads it. He shifts his perspective from speller to reader. He straddles more than one perspective, more than one time and space frame. He is aware not only of a distant audience but also of a distant ideal—that is, the right punctuation, the right spelling, the right cursive letter.

During this stage of their development, children try out rules and experiment with formalities of print. Seven-year-old Peter numbers his pages and puts a period after each number. 'I saw it in a book this way,' he explains. Other late first-graders make two menus for their play restaurant. One is in 'curlicue' for adults, and one is in print for the kids.

Six-year-old Ben adds s-es through his story.

'I liked the way you put an s on for two rabbits,' his teacher said.

'Yup,' Ben answers. He glows with pride. 'One s for two rabbits, two s-es for three rabbits.'

The child's concern with being right does not always lead to the inventiveness and discovery which Ben shows. Annie's mother came to school late in the year and said, 'I used to wish Annie would try to be neat. Now I want the opposite.' The night before, Annie decided to write her Daddy a letter.

'Mommy, will you bring me a piece of paper?'

Annie's mother delivered the paper and Annie began to carefully shape the letters, 'Dear Daddy'. Her pencil slipped. She scrunched the paper up.

'Mommy, I need a new piece.'

Again Annie carefully began to write the heading to her letter. Again she was dissatisfied. This continued for half an hour. Annie never got past her greeting.

One day while Donald Graves was video-taping a six-year-old, the child began to try cursive for the first time. She worked earnestly at her curling letters until a classmate interrupted her. 'You shouldn't do cursive yet,' the child said to the young writer. 'The teacher hasn't showed you yet. You might do it wrong.' The young writer's first steps towards cursive were stymied by the rule-conscious orthodoxy of her classmate. Next time this young writer may not venture into new territory for fear of being wrong. The ability to look ahead to an eventual audience can ruin a child's playful experiments.

Concern With Audience

For Annie, Sarah, and Alex, writing isn't play anymore. They know they have an audience, and knowing this has spoiled their play. Now when Alex spells his words, he puts his letters side by side so they can be read. He keeps his battles little. He doesn't want his drawings to explode into a scrawl. No longer do children write for the sheer play of it. They write to communicate, they write to perform.

The young child who once used dark bold print simply because he remembered the pull of the fishing line now carefully adds exclamation marks and hopes an audience will read it right. For the sake of their audience, children try to choose exciting story topics. 'I'm going to write an adventure story,' Chris announces. 'The kids like adventure stories.' In one third grade room children select topics by listing alternatives and then asking their classmates to vote. Fads spread through third-grade classrooms, where children seem especially audience conscious. Dialogue, sound words (Boom! Ouch!), exclamation marks and favourite topics spread like wildfire. Researcher Susan

Sowers suggests a sociogram of third and fourth grade classrooms might explain some of the topics and techniques children use. She suggests that asking children questions such as 'What three children would you choose as readers for your piece?' might locate the children in the room who have strong influence.

The child at this stage may show his developing ability to write for an audience, to view his work as a product, and to see it through the eyes of a reader by

wanting the paper to be legible
choosing topics based on audience
being concerned with correctness and conventions
anticipating audience response
using popular techniques
anticipating audience needs
looking back on the writing.

Use of Resources

The same time and space changes which contribute to young writers' sense of audience and to their conservatism and concern with correctness can also lead to a new resourcefulness. The child no longer writes in a self-contained cocoon. There is a world out there—a world of resources as well as a world of external judgments, rules and conventions.

Once the child re-invented each word as if it never existed before. Now the same child will say 'Chemicals. Chem-i-cals . . . I know that word. It's on my book.' And the child darts off to fetch a reading book.

When six-year-old Missy wanted to paste bits of bright tissue paper onto the crayoned tree, her plans were blocked by a shortage of tissue paper. Missy gathered together magic marker and Kleenex, and ripped and coloured the Kleenex so as to make her own tissue paper. Missy's invented tissue paper shows a broadening time and space framework. She uses distant materials and she has a sense of controlling time enough to depart from the immediate task of pasting leaves onto her drawing in order to first make tissue paper.

Fetching a spelling word from across the room and gathering materials to make tissue paper are steps toward using reference books, listing information, and interviewing experts. Like a child's early use of resources, these reference skills require the writer to postpone the immediate task of writing in order to tend to a preliminary task. Both require tentativeness, anticipation, planning and pulling together information from disparate perspectives. Reading skills alone do not make children into researchers. Many third graders will dutifully take notes from an encyclopedia and then ignore the notes as they write what they already knew. These children may not have the flexibility and control of time and space which is needed to integrate new information with old, note-taking with reporting.

Ability to Plan Ahead

A child's developing ability to use resources is often accompanied by a growing ability to plan ahead. Both planning and using resources represent an ability to view present time and space in light of a future and a past. Children show their ability to plan in a number of ways.

The role of drawing often changes as children become more able to plan. The child turns to a clean page and picks up a pencil. Once the question, 'What are you going to draw?' would have received the response, 'How should I know, I haven't draw-ed it yet.' Now the child instead dictates the words he plans to write. 'My picture is about "We had snowman snow",' the child says, and begins to draw and write according to plan.

Over-planning a piece can force the discovery out of writing. Professional writers know this and most of them let their pencil lead to new images. Gabriel Fielding says, 'Writing to me is a voyage, an odyssey, a discovery, because I'm never certain of precisely what I will find.' Faulkner describes his writing process this way:

> It begins with a character, usually, and once he stands up on his feet and begins to move, all I do is trot along behind him with a paper and pencil trying to keep up long enough to put down what he says and does.

It is not surprising that when children first develop the ability to plan, they often over-plan. Seven-year-old Scott is convinced that planning everything improves what he has to say.

In an interview at the end of first grade, Chris announced that the first books he'd written aren't as good as his more recent ones. 'I hardly didn't have anything in my head,' he says about his early books. 'I got to the centre of the book and thought of all the information I had to go.' After Scott wrote his early books, he'd think about them at home, come back and cross things out. Now at the end of first grade, Scott is scornful of this process—not realising it is the process most professional writers experience.

Scott claims that lately he thinks about his books beforehand and doesn't have to change them. 'I think about the title. If I start thinking and get the title, then I think of other things. Once I know everything I'm going to write, the next day I can start writing.'

Eventually there will be room for discovery as well as for planning in Scott's writing process. For now, Scott is right to celebrate his new ability to plan. It marks an important step in the progression from play towards craft.

Is This the Writer's Craft?

For many children, the era of exploration and spontaneity is replaced by one of deliberateness, social consciousness, and conformity. Instead of messing about with words, children practise techniques and follow rules. Instead of letting their pencils lead to new images, children carefully pre-plan their writing. Instead of reinventing a new sun each time they paint, children learn to make a spiked round sun in the centre of their sky. Instead of reliving the fish on their line, children question how to convey excitement to their audience. Children no longer write solely for themselves. Writing is no longer all-process, all-present, all-personal. Children are concerned with product and with audience. Writing has 'become conscious of itself as a power of shaping semblances which shall give value for other eyes or ears . . .' Yet, in doing so, writing has lost its playfulness.

Writing Becomes Craft

> The play impulse becomes the art impulse (supposing it is strong enough to survive the play years) when . . . it becomes conscious of itself as a power of shaping semblances which shall give value for other eyes or ears and shall bring recognition and reknowing . . . [*op.cit.*]

Play becomes art *if the playful impulse is strong enough to survive*. Playfulness is part of craft. To experience the cycle of craft, children need a flexible and controlled time and space framework. They need to shift between writing for the sheer play of it and rewriting for audience, correctness, and clarity.

Nine-year-old Amy expects to write many exploratory drafts. 'When I'm on my way to an end, I rush on,' Amy explains. 'I leave things out. I pretend I'm writing the whole story but then I stop and sometimes throw it out and sometimes change it.' Amy's perspective and her process are flexible. Amy knows she can cycle back to a draft and view it from new perspectives, changing what is on the paper.

When Amy wants to become her own reader, she changes her posture and mannerisms. She'll sit up tall, hold the paper away from her face, and mouth each word as she reads it. 'I don't really read it silent or aloud,' she says. 'I read it aloud in my mind.' It's not an abstract process for Amy to become her own reader. It's more like playing dress-up.

Amy says, 'First you write down how you know it'. Then you read it over and you think, 'Can other people understand this?'

As she rereads her draft, she uncovers new memories and images. Amy takes up her pencil and begins to write 'like wildfire'. Reader becomes writer. Critic becomes participant. And, for a while, Amy rediscovers the power of explosions that end in a scrawl.

Summary

Mastery of conventions and concern with audience and final product are part of the process of play becoming craft. But only when the child rediscovers the playful aspects of writing does his composing become like the professional writer's. The all-process, all-personal, all-present framework of the young child is part of the writer's cycle of craft. Once rule-conscious, audience-aware children rediscover their playful roots, their writing process becomes qualitatively similar to the process most professional writers experience.

7. One Child, One Teacher, One Classroom: The Story of One Piece of Writing
Barbara Kamler

JILL WAS IN A SLUMP. She was stuck for a good topic to write about. Her teacher Judy Egan knew it. The last two topics Jill chose had not worked. She was not interested in 'The Day I Changed My Room Around' and she knew nothing about 'Cats'. The result: two stories lacking in detail and interest for both reader and writer. In the writing conference, Jill did not respond to her teacher's questions about content. She had little information to add to either piece. At the conclusion of the conference, the soft-spoken woman broached the issue of topic by first empathising with Jill's problem:

Mrs E: It really is easier to write if you have a lot of information about a topic. I can tell in your book that you've had a little bit of difficulty describing things because you don't really have a cat to watch. It would be very easy for me to write this book *Cats* because I have a cat and I could watch it all the time.

Jill: (mournfully) I can't.

Mrs E: That's right, you can't. I can tell you'd really like to have a cat though. That's rather obvious to me.

Together, child and teacher brainstormed writing topics. They talked about what had been happening at home for Jill. They consulted the inside left cover of Jill's writing folder for 'Some New Ideas To Write About' and found the following list:

1. Washington, D.C.
2. Florida
3. Hershey Park
4. My Bird

When Jill showed most interest in talking about her bird, Gus, Egan followed her lead, exploring the possibilities of the topic and stressing the potential contribution to Jill's readers: 'How many people in this room do you think would know what a cockateil is?' It then came out that Jill already had written about this topic in September. Egan proposed that Jill write the new book without consulting the old, so that when she completed it, she could compare the two to see her improvement. Jill was excited by the challenge. She squealed that she could definitely make this book better.

Egan knew her seven year old writer well. She is a sensitive observer of the twenty-one children in her second grade classroom at Atkinson Academy, a public school in rural New Hampshire. Egan watches to learn how these children change over time in their writing processes. Because she observes, she is responsive. I entered this responsive environment in January, 1980, to study children's writing processes. This paper describes the full context in which one child developed one piece of writing; more accurately, it follows the learning and teaching processes that allowed one piece of writing to evolve.

I had observed Jill for a week before her conference about her cockateil. I was as excited as Jill and anticipated the growth I would see in her as a writer. I went to the master file where Egan maintains a collection of all the children's writing and drafts from entry on the first day of school to the end of the year, and found Jill's five-page illustrated September edition of her bird book.

Jill's Text	Egan's Transcription*
Ear Brid On My Mtethr Anivrsire	*Our Bird On My Mother's Anniversary*
1. We got a bird for my moms and Tom anivrsire. it is il difrit cilrs. my sistr rathr have a hoos. and i rathr have a bipe	We got a bird for my mom's and Tom's anniversary. It is all different colours. My sister would rather have a horse. I'd rather have a puppy.
2. ear bird wacs me up. he wisil to mich	Our bird wakes me up. He whistles too much.
3. we gat youst to it. he is a coklt. You no how theu ear.	We got used to it. He is a cockateil. You know how they are.

*Jill's words are copied into adult spelling to help Egan remember the exact message.

4. He stass on top of the dor or he stas on hes cag

    He stays on top of the door or he stays on his cage.

5. Abou the author

it is a chro store I like to sce I like scrl his neam is Gus

    About the Author

This is a true story. Jill likes to ski and she likes school. Jill's bird's name is Gus.

That was September. It was now March. Jill had her topic, chose her writing materials and began her new book on March 6, completing it the morning of March 7. Dark head resting on left elbow, nose two inches from the page, she wrote in rapid bursts, with frequent stops in between. She held her pencil loosely; it seemed to float across the page. She made two trips into the hall and continually shuffled the papers in her writing folder. I observed no signs of concentration. She paid little attention to spelling and handwriting, much attention to interruptions. Twenty minutes after she had begun, this brown-eyed, elfish child stood abruptly. She closed the cover of her unlined book, returned her pencil to the orange caddy that held all writing implements, went to the window sill and placed her book in an orange bucket labelled 'READY FOR A CONFERENCE'. She then placed her writing folder in the orange bucket marked 'WRITING FOLDERS'. She returned to the work board and paused. She considered going into either the Pretend area to work on the maple syrup project or the Art area to complete her kite, but finally decided on the Listening area. She moved her name tag from 'Writing' to 'Listening', and settled into a Robert McCloskey tape of *Blueberries For Sal*.

I was stunned. Was that it? The writer I had just observed seemed careless and uninterested, scribbling words quickly to be done with it. I needed to check my perception against her draft. I took her book from the conference bucket and read the following story:

DRAFT I March 7

My Bird on My Mom's and Tom's Aniversire

Page 1. My Bide is a coktel He cherps all day. Chip

      (My Bird is a cockateil. He chirps all day. Chirp.)*

2. A coktel is funny looking Thay look a libt bit like

      (A cockateil is funny looking. They look a little bit like . . .)

3. I made a mastake on Pacg the 2

      (I made a mistake on this page 2.)

4. My sestr rather have a hows insted.

      (My sister would rather have a horse instead.)

5. I love my bird

6. My brid side to saye good By.

      (My bird said to say, 'Goodbye'.)

7. t h e

      n

      d

---

*I have transcribed Jill's text for ease of reading.

It did not look promising. There was no detail, nothing of interest about the bird. I looked at the September version which was certainly more legible and coherent; it contained more information and the handwriting was more controlled. Discouraged, I was reduced to counting words: 57 words in March, 88 in September. Words like *lazy* and *careless* came to mind—skimpy and general. I was negative and could only see what the story was not and what the child had not done.

Judy Egan, on the other hand, did not treat the piece as a final product. She was as unimpressed as I by the content and aware that the book has not been reread or checked, so it was ready for a conference. But she was not negative. The book in the conference bucket was not there to be evaluated and marked. It was there to be conferenced, listened to, developed. Egan's process of teaching makes room for each child's process of writing. She provides a structure for the young learner's efforts, yet leaves room for the individual's style and pace.

The whole classroom is structured to this end. The room is divided into independent learning areas—listening, writing, reading, pretend, blocks, science, math. Egan spends time introducing the children to and familiarising them with the self-directed activities in each of the areas. Through conference and share sessions she helps children learn how to use the learning materials wisely and responsibly. There is a depth of activity for children to be involved in, an organisation which encourages independent choice. She is a teacher who believes in responsible choice and responsible action.

Consistent with this external structure, there is a writing process structure which is part of the internal organisation of the classroom. When children complete a piece of writing, they are scheduled for individual writing conferences. In a conference, the teacher listens to a child read and together they work on the content and skills. The teacher keeps a log of the conference. When four stories have been completed and conferenced, the child chooses one for publication. In a small group conference, child writers react to one another's chosen piece and then work on the final revision of their own piece. After the book is typed by a parent volunteer, the child completes the publishing cycle by illustrating each page, binding the wallpapered cardboard book cover and sharing the published book with the whole class. The book is then added to the collection of stories in the classroom library.

Jill's bird book was the third of her current publishing cycle, and one she eventually chose to publish. During the publishing cycle that I observed, Jill wrote and revised four books and two poems; she participated in eight writing conferences and shared two published books with the whole class. The timetable below indicates only the chronology of processes directly related to her bird book.

March   6—Begins composing *My Bird on My Mom's and Tom's Anniversary.*

March   7—Completes composing.

March 11—Conference with Debbie (a peer). Makes Draft II revisions.

March 11—Conference with Egan. Makes Draft III revisions.
March 13—Skills conference with Egan. Makes Draft IV revisions.
March 21—Group Conference. Makes Draft V revisions.
March 24—Illustrates book. Binds book.
March 25—Shares book with whole class. Book enters class library.

On March 11, Jill was one of six children scheduled for a writing conference. The morning began as usual with all the children planning their morning activities on the rug. Some went to the pretend corner to work on their puppet show, others to the library and reading area, and a third group to the writing table. At Egan's direction, Jill and the other conferees went to the language table. Egan had requested that Jill first spend time with seven-year-old Debbie going over the book to be sure it was ready for a conference. Debbie and Jill were friends and knew each other well. Egan hoped this peer conference, like the three others going on at the same time in the room, would help Jill add more information and provide groundwork for the teacher-child conference to follow.

The girls were confident and seemed to know how to proceed; certainly they had had excellent, consistent modelling from their teacher. Jill began by reading each page aloud to Debbie. Removed from the piece for four days, Jill's eyes became more critical. She had trouble deciphering some of her content and later confided to Egan, 'Me and Debbie couldn't even understand it!', to which her non-jugmental teacher replied, 'You're kidding! You wrote it and you couldn't understand it! That happens.'

As Jill listened to her own words, she made changes on pages 1, 2 and 3 without any prompting or comment from Debbie, and on pages 4, 5 and 8 in direct response to questions Debbie asked. The draft below focuses on the relationship between the content of this writing conference and Jill's subsequent activity in changing the draft. In every case throughout the process, Jill made *all* changes on the original March 7 draft; she never recopied the whole story. I have shown all changes from Draft I by writing them in by hand.

DRAFT II March 11

My Bird on My Mom's and Tom's Anivesire

Jill's Text After Conference	*Conference Questions and Behaviours*
Page 1. My bide is a coktel He cherps all day Chip **Chip.**	Debbie does not comment or ask questions. Jill makes these changes as she goes along reading each page.
2. A coktel is funny looking Thay look **nothing** like **this**	
3. ~~I made a mastake on Paeg the 2~~	

4. My sestr rather have a
   hows insted

   **bcis the bid crips well
   we are watching t.v.**

5. ~~I love my bird~~

D: My sister rather have a
    horse. Why is that there?

J: Because the bird chirps
    while we're watching t.v.

D: Why do you love your
    bird?

J: Because . . . I don't know
    why I love my bird.
    (Crosses out sentence.)

6. My brid side to saye
   good By.

7. T h e
      n
      d

8. **Aobt the Ater

   My bird is name Gus

   has name is rele

   Agstis**

D: Are you going to put
    about the author? (The
    last page of each book
    contains a statement about
    the author that is written
    by the child.)

At the conclusion of this half hour conference, Jill had made six content changes which affected the overall meaning of the piece. She had deleted information which made no sense or which she could not support; she added information to clarify or explain. Debbie's presence was crucial to the content revisions of the draft. Her physical presence forced Jill to reread the book for the first time since composing; Debbie seemed to make the concept of audience visible for Jill. Jill also needed an active reader to ask questions. Debbie was attentive and encouraging; when Jill showed her the page-four revisions, Debbie giggled and made quick little claps for her friend. Jill was open to her suggestions, never defensive. She was in control, choosing to respond to some of Debbie's questions, to ignore others. She shared some of her problems in writing the book ('I had pictures but I scribbled them out because they're awful'.) and tried to keep the focus on her own work ('Come on, Debbie, we're supposed to be doing mine.').

Four days earlier, Jill had dumped the story in the conference bucket without looking back. Now she seemed to be reclaiming responsibility for the piece. When she had completed the content changes, she attended to her proofreading duties. 'I have to check everything on my folder,' she told Debbie as she consulted the list of 'THINGS JILL CAN DO'. The list was compiled in conference by Jill and her teacher when both noted that a particular skill was used successfully:

1. Put title on folder
2. Put title on book
3. Put date
4. Put first and last name
5. Number pages
6. Use periods

7. Use *?*
8. Use Part I and Part II
9. Use 'too'
10. Use 'er' like in brother

She went through her story systematically checking each page against the list on her folder. She saw no further changes to make and announced loudly: 'Ready for a conference!' It was Jill speaking, but I heard the now internalised voice of her teacher, patiently asking each child at the beginning of each conference: 'Are you ready for a conference? Have you checked the back of your folder to be sure you are ready?'

Jill put her story in the teacher's conference log and placed it on the corner of Egan's child-sized conference table, especially ordered because it is small, private and conducive to focusing attention. Jill went to her cubby for a piece of cake, then to the window where she and Debbie shared the cake, talking, laughing, arms around each other. Then Debbie claimed her time: 'O.K., Jill, you help me now!' They reversed roles, returned to the language table to work on Debbie's book, *Ice Follies,* until Mrs Egan was ready to see Jill twenty minutes later.

Jill was proud to report the results of her conference with Debbie, 'I had six things to change and she had four.' With one arm resting on the back of Jill's chair, Egan shared the child's enthusiasm: 'Wow! Six things! I'd like to see what they are! Read it to me and tell me about the changes you've made.' This was Jill's second writing conference that morning, her teacher's fourth. Egan began positively, as always, accepting the child and her piece of work as something valuable, something she had worked hard on, something worth listening to. She affirmed what the child could do, then shifted to areas of weakness.

The problem: a skimpy story about a bird named Gus. The focus: how to get the child to add information. The result: a thirty minute conference. Egan didn't know the conference would last this long when she began. She did know that Jill was in a slump and that time spent on developing content would be worthwhile; she did know her room, at this time of year, was capable of running itself. When she saw the fruits of the conference, she knew from previous experience that the time spent was justified, the effects for Jill long lasting.

Egan began the conference by intensively probing the content with Jill. She was at first very directive. Egan asked many questions about the bird's physical appearance, his habitat, his diet. For ten minutes she controlled the discussion, pushing Jill to talk about her bird Gus. She took the role of naive reader, one who knew nothing about the bird, when in fact Egan did know about the bird and Jill knew it. This was a conscious decision on her part. She believes Jill enjoys the back and forth bantering, the parley. Jill's replies were abbreviated; if anything, Egan did more talking. The interchange was fast and quick, punctuated by laughter, high spirits and Jill's occasional exasperation.

Mrs E: Where do you keep a cockateil?
Jill: In a cage!
Mrs E: Like Munchkin? (resident guinea pig)
Jill: No. A bird cage.
Mrs E: Oh! A bird cage!
Jill: You know that! (exasperated)
Mrs E: But if I were a person who didn't know what a cockateil was, I
       might be confused by that.
Jill: Mmmm. (tolerant)
Mrs E: Think now, Jill, about Gus. Does he always stay in the cage?
Jill: No.
Mrs E: No?
Jill: Of course not! He got *bit* by the dog!
Mrs E: You're kidding! The dog bit him?
Jill: Yeah! He ate one of the feathers and then threw up.
       (voice becoming higher and more animated)
Mrs E: Oh, no! So Gus gets out of the cage on purpose.
       Do you let him out? Or is it a mistake?
Jill: No! The dog comes in the den, and now he knows not to come
       in when the bird's on the floor.
Mrs E: Now let me get this straight. The bird comes out of the cage
       because you want it to come out of the cage. You open the
       door?
Jill: He has a choice.
Mrs E: You mean he knows how to open the door?
Jill: No, *we* open the door!
Mrs E: Alright. You ask Gus if he wants to come out and if he does he
       comes out of the door.
Jill: No. It's his choice.
Mrs E: So you just leave the door open and he . . .
Jill: (not letting her finish) YEAH!

For ten minutes they discussed details of the bird in this manner.
Then it was time for Jill to decide what information to add to the
book. Egan did not decide. She guided Jill's selection process. The
directive, pushing teacher began to move back from her position of
control so that she could return responsibility for the writing to the
child. At the end of the morning Jill had made extensive content
additions and developed her story further. Once again, I have shown
all changes from Draft II by writing them in by hand. The relationship
between the content of this conference and the changes Jill made in
her book is more complex than the relationship described in the peer
conference. Excerpts from the conference that are related to Draft III
changes are posted in the right-hand column. Note how Egan
gradually transfers responsibility to the child in the conference:

DRAFT III March 11

My Bird on My Mom's and Tom's Anivesire

Jill's Text After Conference   *Related Conference Dialogue*

Page 1. My bide is a coktel He
         cherps all day "Chip
         Chip."

(My bird is a cockateil.
He chirps all day. 'Chirp
Chirp.')

2. A coktel is funny
looking
~~Thay look nothing like this~~
**bcis he has feters
steking up and win
he is yiang his fias
is gray and win his
oldr his feas ges yelur**

(A cockateil is funny
looking because he has
feathers sticking up and
when he is young his
face is gray and when
he's older his face goes
yellow.)

2a. **My bird hade's
vidmins in his widr
I think it is funne
don't you? and
his food is
Sunflowr ses
and gafl and
parti seds**

(My bird has vitamins
in his water. I think it
is funny don't you? and
his food is sunflower
seeds and gravel and
parrot seeds.)

3. **Own fon nite the
brid frou out fo
the den and the
dog bit the bird
and the bird din't
did but the dog
at one of the
beds feters
and he th up.**

Mrs E: I know quite a few
reasons why this is a
funny looking bird.
What are some of those
reasons?

Teacher initiates summing up.
Teacher nominates physical
appearance of bird as topic, but
asks child to recall detail. No
prompting. Teacher asks child to
make additions to page 2 at
conference table. After child
rereads additions aloud, teacher
asks: 'Do you want to leave this
sentence, "The bird looks
nothing like this?"'

Mrs E: Alright, Jill, now think
of some of the other
things we've talked
about just now about
your cockateil.

Jill: Food.

Mrs E: Food. All right. Where
would be a good place to
fit it in?

Teacher initiates more general
revision question. Child
nominates food as topic. Teacher
does not ask child to recall
relevant details. Teacher directs
attention to problems of
sequence and physical space.
Teacher asks child to make
additions at conference table.

Mrs E: Are there any other
places you think you
need to work on?

Jill: I love my bird. I crossed
that out because I don't
know why I love him.

Mrs E: Think about that for a
minute . . . You would be
upset if you didn't have
your bird.

Jill: I know. I know what I
could add!

Mrs E: What?

(One fine night the bird flew out of the den and the dog bit the bird and the bird didn't die but the dog ate one of the bird's feathers and he threw up.)

Jill: When the dog jumped and *BIT* the bird!

Teacher's open-ended question asks child to take more responsibility. Child decided topic and content detail. She temporarily ignores teacher's question to initiate her own content addition. Child is gaining control. Teacher directs child to language table to make additions independently. Child returns to reread after she completed changes.

4. My sest(er)rather have a hows insted bcis the bid crips well we are wiching t.v.

(My sister rather have a horse instead because the bird chirps while we are watching t.v.)

Child initiates change. Rereads page 2 additions aloud and proclaims:

Jill: I put an 'er.'

Mrs E: I was glad to see you used 'er' in 'feather.' How about on 'sister?'

Although teacher directs focus to word 'sister,' unlikely change would have been made at this time if child had not initiated.

5. **I love my brid bcus he is nice to me**

(I love my bird because he is nice to me.)

Refer to conference dialogue for page 3 above.

6. My brid side to saye good By
(My bird said to say, 'Goodbye.')

7. T h e
      n
      d

8. Aobt the Ater
My bird is name Gus
has name is rele Agstis
(About the Author. My bird is named Gus. His name is really Augustus.)

Throughout this interchange, Jill depended on Egan as audience to push and help develop the content of the book. As the conference proceeded, she gradually took the initiative, selecting and choosing which information she would add. Jill seemed charged by the conference. She proudly showed Debbie her new content additions and then returned to the conference table to wait for her teacher, who had been helping Sean and Andy with dinosaur research in the science corner. Jill's behaviour loudly proclaimed that she felt in control. She wrote a quick poem, put it in her writing folder and said: 'Another one. Now I'm ready for publishing.'

She was on top, but at every step of the way, her teacher helped her gain that sense of control through skilful conferencing. Egan has high expectations: she asks her children to be responsible for their actions and their writing. She always begins with the positive, affirming what the children can do, rather than dwelling on what they can't. She always consults; she asks rather than tells. In this way she guides children to maintain control of their writing and live up to their responsibilities as writers.

The next morning, Judy Egan scheduled a second conference with Jill on the bird book so that she could work with her on some skills in context. Jill began by reading her freshly revised book aloud to her teacher and concluded: 'It's better than the first copy because I added more.' She made the following corrections/additions at this time:

DRAFT IV March 13
> *My Bird on My Mom's and Tom's Aniversire*

Page 1. My bide is a coktel He cherps all day **on the door**
~~"Chip Chip"~~

2. oldr → older
2a. widr → wider
    sunflr → sunflower
6. side → said
    added quotation marks to *goodbye.*

The conference lasted 18 minutes. During that time, Jill made only four spelling corrections. The bulk of the conference was devoted to teaching, to revising and reinforcing skills. Egan gave her student time. She sat close to Jill and treated all errors positively: 'Look at the word *said*. That's a word you use quite a bit now that you're using quotation marks. You've got many of the letters that are in *said* right here in your word. It does have four letters. Can you hear what comes at the beginning?' As Jill has used contractions, apostrophes and question marks correctly in her book, Egan started there; she spent a lot of time asking Jill to apply her knowledge of contractions to new contexts. Egan's entry in Jill's conference log book that day gives a better sense of what transpired than the changes in the actual draft:

3-13 *My Bird . . .*
Reinforced 'er' on *water, sunflower, older*
Used 'er' on *rather, feather, sister*
Sp. of *said*
Used *look* correctly—hadn't on spelling test
Used ' on *didn't.* Applied ' to *don't*
Used *?*

The last five minutes of the conference were very exciting for Jill. Egan took Jill's September bird book from the master file. The challenge Jill had accepted a week earlier was to make her March bird book better. Now the time for comparison was here. Jill read her earlier work aloud to her teacher. Her reactions to the text made several aspects of her growth and expectations as a writer visible to me.

First, she had great trouble reading the book, particularly deciphering her own spelling. On more than one occasion she abandoned her own words and read her teacher's transcription instead. Amazed, she said, 'I don't believe this page . . . I don't believe I spelled *got* that way.' Her spelling had changed. So too had her expectations about a book's content. On reading the last page, she turned the book over, said, 'Huh?' and looked for another page of information. She was surprised there was no more. She thought the book was short and that there should have been more content—even though her first draft of the current bird book contained less information than the September version. Her concept of writing had changed. Now she treated the initial composing as first draft, as a frame to hold the barest outline of ideas. She had learned that the conference process would help her fill out that outline and move beyond the bare essentials.

Another look at her September book showed me that Jill had not made content revisions and that her writing was neater, more controlled. Her March book was, by contrast, anything but neat. Jill was very impressed with the messiness of her book. On several occasions, she proudly compared it to an earlier book, *Earrings,* which was a breakthrough for Jill in revising: when 'messy' became a positive term associated with change; when how the book looked became less important than what was said. At that point, her words began to flow, her content to improve.

Holding both books in her hand, she returned to the language table at the peak of control over her writing. When she asked Katy to compare the two books and received an unsatisfactory answer, she proclaimed knowingly: 'It has more information. I don't like it. It's not my best. It might have been my best then, but it isn't now.' She completed her changes on the book, checked them with Egan, wrote a note to her teacher asking that she assign her to the writing area the following morning, took stock of her writing folder and put a big 'NO' on the cover of 'Cats', thus ruling it out for publication. Although she had worked steadily for over an hour, Jill took a new booklet to the writing table and began writing a special publication on author, Shel Silverstein.

Eight days later, on March 21, Jill met with Tracey, Andy and Mrs Egan for a group publishing conference. Jill had not been idle during the intervening week. She had finished writing another book and participated in one large group conference, one peer conference and two teacher conferences. Now she and Tracey and Andy were meeting with Mrs Egan to make their nominated book better. Quality was important; making things better was part of the publishing process. The children were familiar with the structure. They would be asked to tell why their book was the best and why they had chosen it. They would read their books to one another, listening to the feedback they received so they could later decide what final changes to make. In turn, they would be expected to be good listeners, to ask questions of one another, to seek clarification where necessary.

Jill was a very active listener in this conference. She questioned Andy and Tracey about their stories in a demanding and straightforward manner. Like her model, Judy Egan, she did not settle for general responses: she wanted specifics. When she was dissatisfied with an answer from Andy, she was demanding of him: 'No. I want to know why he's happy, not why he looks happy.' As a recipient of feedback, Jill was more defensive. She firmly defended her text when she felt her information was correct:

Mrs Egan: Tracey, do you think in 'About the Author' is the best place for Jill to have that information about Gus's name?

Tracey: No.

Mrs Egan: Are you happy with that information being in 'About the Author', Jill?

Jill: Yes.

Mrs Egan: Why did you put it there instead of putting it in the actual story?

Jill: Because I usually do that because it's going to wreck the book if I say, 'My bird is named Augustus but his name . . .', so I put it in 'About the Author.'

Tracey: You could say why you call him Gus now and Augustus later.

Jill: I want it in the author!

Although not always open to questions or comments from Tracey or Andy, Jill did listen when she felt a proposed change might add to her book. At the conclusion of the conference, she made these additional content changes:

DRAFT V March 21

My Bird on My Mom's and Tom's Aniversire

Page 3. Own fon nite the brid frou out fo the den and the dog bit the brid and the brid din't did but the dog at one of the beds feters and he th up. *The dog side "Grrrrrrrer" at the bard.*

(One fine night the bird flew out of the den and the dog bit the bird and the bird didn't die but the dog ate one of the bird's feathers and he threw up. The dog said, "Grrrrrrrer" at the bird.)

8. Aobt the Ater My bird is name Gus Has name is rele Agstis *On my mom's annivrside we got a bard.*

(About the Author My bird is named Gus. His name is really Augustus. On my mom's anniversary we got a bird.)

Jill seemed tired at the end of the conference, perhaps the cumulative exhaustion of adding so much information to her story.

She chose a flowered book cover for the book and wandered around the classroom with it tucked under her arm for ten minutes. Then she returned to the window sill, rejected the flower cover and chose instead a more modest gold fleck pattern. She placed her book inside the cover and placed the whole in the orange bucket marked, 'READY FOR PUBLISHING'.

A parent volunteer typed the book over the weekend. On Monday morning, March 24, Judy Egan proudly returned the book to her hardworking writer. Jill looked unsettled. She did not want to illustrate the book. She wanted to go to art to start a new art project. She looked dissatisfied as she reread her book on the rug. She claimed there was a typing error on page six. When Mrs. Egan offered to have the page retyped, Jill declined.

She moved into the hallway to a long rectangular table where she joined Tommy illustrating *Shel Silverstein,* Kim illustrating *My Brother's Scary Attempt For an Accident,* and Hilary writing *My Doll Collection.* I did not expect Jill to take much time with her illustrations. She had used only the barest line drawings on her first draft, and on a number of occasions during the cycle, I had heard her complain about her lack of ability at drawing. The care and detail she gave to her illustrations astounded me. She carefully coloured each word in her title with a different coloured marker. Her attention to detail on page 1 was meticulous. She portrayed not only the interior of her den with the bird sitting on the door, but also showed the sky, bushes, trees, clouds, sun, and dog house visible through the glass door in the den.

When she stopped to prepare for lunch, she had taken 55 minutes to illustrate only the first two pages. The patience she showed in her drawing contrasted directly with her verbal behaviour toward the other children at the table. She was aggressive, at times offensive. She called Michael, 'Fat Face', because he was using the marker she wanted, to which he replied, 'No wonder your sister doesn't let you play with her friends.' When Kim accidentally knocked Jill's hand, Jill slammed her hand on the table yelling, 'KIM! KIM!', in her most reprimanding tone.

The illustrating was demanding. She began in marker, then wanted to change to coloured pencil: 'I want to do coloured pencils, not markers, 'cause I stink at birds and I stink at couches.' But she perceived the change as a problem. She sought counsel from Hilary: 'Hilary, do you think if I did this page in marker I could do the rest in coloured pencil?', and finally seemed consoled by Hilary's response: 'Yeah, it's OK. I've seen real published books go from pen and ink to watercolour.'

Until then, I had observed Jill glorifying mess, never neatness. Now I observed her concentrating, doing careful, detailed work. She was capable of both and knew when each was appropriate for her purposes. But the concentrating seemed to take its toll. I wondered if it had anything to do with her irritability. She completed her illustrations that afternoon.

On March 25 Jill shared her book with the whole class. Her 57-word first draft of March 7 had grown to 169 words. I have number-coded and divided the final typed version of Jill's story to indicate at which point in the writing process Jill added the information.

Jill had worked hard. As I thought back over the extensive additions she had made in four conferences, I felt a sense of accomplishment. I was surprised at her behaviour when she shared her published book with the whole group. I had expected to hear the lively, squeaky voice, the expressive reader I had heard at all stages of the publishing cycle. Instead, she read softly, mumbled words, lost her place, and dropped the book on the floor. This, according to Egan, was typical of her behaviour at all stages of the process earlier in the year. Now it seemed confined to the large group situation.

Exposing herself before this group was like asking, 'Well, what do you think of *it?* What do you think of *me?*' Earlier in the publishing cycle, she had relied on her audience as part of the process. She enjoyed the banter and joking, the challenges and changing. She was excited, responsive, in control. Yet when she placed the book in the publishing bucket, the process seemed to end for her; she lost control. The book became final and separate. She experienced her audience on

My Bird on My Mom's and Tom's Anniversary

Page 1. ① My bird is a Cockateil.
He chirps all day │ on the door. ④

2. My bird has vitamins in his water.
I think it is funny, don't you?
His food is sunflower seeds and gravel
and parrot seeds. ③

3. ① A cockateil is funny looking │ because
he has feathers sticking up and when he's young, ③
his face is gray and when he's older, his
face is yellow.

4. One fine night the bird flew out of the den
and the dog bit the bird and the bird didn't ③
die but the dog pulled out some of the bird's
feathers and he threw up. │ The dog said ⑤
"Grrrrrrrrrrer" at the bird.

5. My sister would rather have a horse instead ①
because the bird chirps while we are watching ②
t.v.

6. ① I love my bird │ because he is nice to me. ③

7. My bird said to say "Goodbye". ①

8. The End. ①

9. *About the Author*
My bird is named Gus. ②
His name is really Augustus.
On my Mom's anniversary, we got a bird. ⑤

① Initial Composing. Draft I — March 7
② Conference with Debbie. Draft II Revisions — March 11
③ Conference with Egan. Draft III Revisions — March 11
④ Conference with Egan. Draft IV Revisions — March 13
⑤ Group Conference. Draft V Revisions — March 21

a different level: before, as challenger and prober, now, as critic and judge. Despite the positive nature of the sharing—Jill chose the people she wanted to comment on her book and everyone knew they must share what they liked about it—Jill retreated. She was flushed and embarrassed. Jill was a child of process, not product. The information she offered to the group during the sharing confirmed this perception. She made sure to tell the class she had spent the 'WHOLE MORNING' illustrating page one; she went to the master file for her draft copy so she could show the class *all* the changes she had made and the resulting messiness of her draft: process news.

Jill's published product entered the class library on March 25 where it joined over a hundred other published works by the child writers of Egan's second grade class. The title was entered on the 'Rockwell Publishing Company' chart of published works, posted outside the door of the classroom. The books listed beside Jill's name now read as follows: (1) *Squeaky and Me,* (2) *A Trip,* (3) *Stitches,* (4) *Earrings,* (5) *My Puppy,* (6) *My Bird on My Mom's and Tom's Anniversary.*

As I looked again at Jill's published book, I was not overly impressed. The book was interesting but ordinary. It was certainly not the best published piece Jill had done that year. She had written it at a time when she was stuck for topics and just coming out of her slump. The book was a book; the child, a child. No miracles. No child prodigy. The product told little. The extraordinary thing was the process, a process that gave Jill room to pull herself out of a rut; a process that helped her develop an inadequate beginning into a competent end; a process that allowed her to emerge from the completion of one publishing cycle, recharged for the next.

Egan's classroom environment allowed Jill to experience her own writing process and develop as a writer. Jill remained in control because Egan allowed her to do so. Jill chose her writing materials, her paper and pencil, her topic for writing. Jill determined the time spent composing, the number of interruptions she would allow or encourage. Guided through an extensive conference process, Jill decided what changes would be made. Jill chose the book she would publish, the cover the book would be bound in; she controlled the illustration process. She worked with a teacher who put the responsibility on the child writer.

In such an environment, Jill the writer had no illusions about the difficulty of writing. She knew it took time and hard work. She knew that everything she wrote would not be her best, that expectations of perfection during the early stages were unrealistic. She was learning to value revision. Her behaviour during the publishing cycle indicated that she had come to value process over product.

On Tuesday, March 25, Jill concluded her publishing cycle. On March 26 her writing folder was empty. On March 27, she had a morning conference with Egan about poetry and wrote a poem, 'Pussywillows,' which was published and displayed that afternoon. The same day, she shared her *Shel Silverstein* book with the whole class and began a new book. She chose the title, *At Home Is Fun,* scribbled some ideas. She was ready to write.

8. When Children Want to Punctuate: Basic Skills Belong in Context

Lucy McCormick Calkins

THE RECENT NATIONAL CONCERN WITH WRITING comes at a bad time. Teachers are stretched too thin. They've already squeezed courses on health, computers, drug abuse and careers into their curriculum. 'We've become adept at multiplication and addition,' Donald Graves says, 'and we've forgotten all about subtraction and division.' It's no wonder teachers are asking, 'Where am I to get the time—and the energy—to teach writing?'

What teachers don't realise is that writing brings energy into the curriculum. The urge to tell leads children to struggle with punctuation and language mechanics. 'I want to publish my mini-bike report. Will you help me make it perfect?' 'How can I make the wicked robot groan and yell?' When children write, they reach for the skills they need.

When children ask the questions and raise the dilemmas, skills are learned in context. But this requires a pace which is qualitatively different from most of American education. 'I like working on my pieces and making them better and better,' nine year old Andrea says, 'but I need to have all the time I want. If a teacher says, 'You have to get this done in a week,' you write fast and don't want to see mistakes or try new things. You're afraid to find that it's not good, not what you wanted.

Young writers need time to run into their own problems, to ask their own questions. Only then can skills be learned in context—for the context is not the subject matter, but the child's question, the child's need.

Writing takes time. And that time has to come from somewhere else in the curriculum. At Atkinson Academy, a public school in rural New Hampshire, teachers at every grade level take time from formal language instruction and give it to writing.

'Letting go of the drills and workbook exercises felt like a gamble,' Ms Beth Hoban says. 'I was scared my third graders wouldn't learn mechanics.' But Ms Hoban figured the only way to find what writing could do was to give it time—lots of time. 'We write for an hour a day, three days a week,' she says.

Ms West—the teacher across the hall—didn't take the writing gamble. She continued to teach language mechanics through daily drills and workbook exercises. 'I start at the very beginning, teaching them simple sentences, periods, capitals,' she explains. 'Everything that is in the book, I do a whole lesson on it.' Ms West writes sentences on the chalkboard and asks her children to insert the missing punctuation. She makes dittos on question marks and gives pre-tests and post-tests on periods. Her children rarely write.

Both teachers say, 'I begin at the very beginning.' For Ms West, the beginning is the declarative sentence and the rules of using periods. For Beth Hoban, the beginning is the child's information, the child's desire to be seen and heard. Both teachers believe in basic skills. One teaches them in isolation, the other teaches them in context.

Ms Hoban's gamble paid off. Because her children invented and used punctuation for their own purposes, they learned it more effectively than if they were doing drills, workbook exercises, and language lessons.

Researcher Lucy Calkins documented this. For a year, she observed Hoban's children each day while they wrote. She also interviewed all the children in Ms Hoban's and Ms West's classrooms.

'Do you like punctuation?' 'What's it good for?' Calkins asked children from both rooms. Then she showed each child fourteen different kinds of punctuation. 'What's this for?' she asked as she drew a semicolon, an apostrophe.

The third grade 'writers' who had not had formal instruction in punctuation could define/explain an average of 8.66 kinds of punctuation. The children who had studied punctuation through classwork, drills and tests, but had rarely written, were only able to define/explain 3.85 kinds of punctuation.

Writers Need Punctuation: Their Audience

'Will you read my fishing piece,' Alan says to his friend. 'I want to put it in a book.' They pull their chairs up to a desk in the back of the room. Jennie falters as she begins to read the story. 'Read it better,' Alan says. 'Come on ... when they talk, read it out like a conversation.' But Jennie can't, not without punctuation. So they find a red pencil and put commas and quotation marks into the draft.

Later, Alan sends a copy of his fishing story to the school paper, and he puts the final draft on display, along with his fishing gear. Children in Beth Hoban's classroom know their writing will be read by classmates, and they want it to be clear. 'If you want your story to make sense, you can't write without punctuation,' Alan says now. 'Punctuation tells people things—like if the sentence is asking, or if someone is talking, or if you should yell it out.'

Chip agrees. Readers need punctuation. 'It lets you know where the sentence ends, so otherwise one minute you'd be sledding down the hill and the next minute you're inside the house, without even stopping.'

In the first grade at Atkinson, where children also write and write for each other, it is often their sense of audience which prompts them to use punctuation. For young children, writing usually begins as a kind of egocentric play. They write for the sheer fun of it, with no thought to an eventual audience. Children at this stage aren't much interested in punctuation. Later, as they become aware of their audience, they begin to look over their print, asking, 'Will they be able to read this?' Six-year-old Becky watched two boys peer down at her page.

'What's this say?' they asked.

Becky had run her words together, without leaving spaces between them. Now she adds dashes to separate words. Oftentimes young writers use punctuation for unorthodox reasons. No one corrected Becky's use of the dash. Adult 'mistakes' are often a child's step forward. Becky's teacher encourages children to experiment with punctuation, to solve their own problems. Later, if Becky doesn't stop separating words with dashes, her teacher will suggest she leave spaces instead of dashes.

Third graders, like younger children, often misuse punctuation when they first use it. 'I never take points off for it,' Beth Hoban says. 'I want them to try new things, to solve their own problems.'

Children in the writing classrooms connect punctuation with writing and with reading each other's writing. And they like it.

Fewer than twenty-five percent of the children in the 'mechanics' classroom like punctuation. 'Punctuation is embarrassing,' one nine year old in this class says. 'I'd like it if I were good at it, but I'm not,' a classmate adds. 'You forget what it's for,' a third says.

Writers don't forget what punctuation is for. It is for their audience, and it is for their voice.

Writers Need Punctuation: Their Voice

Print is a silent language. Children want to give voice to their stories. They want their print to speak out loud. Very young children often put expression into their print by darkening important syllables or capitalising some words for emphasis. When six-year-old Brad put the word *pull* in his story, he went back to the word and carefully darkened each of the letters.

'Why'd you do that?' Don Graves asked.

Brad looked up at him. 'Because I want them to know to really PULL!'"

But young children soon find that patches and strings of big and small, loopy tight letters do not translate into the lilt of a reader's voice. Amy's friend squints and struggles over Amy's dinosaur story. Amy sees this, and hears her faltering version of the tale. How can she make her friend's voice hang, expectantly, before a list of dinosaur names? How can she direct the voice to *crash?* How can she make it soften and grow harsh?

Step by step, Amy begins to learn conventional markers which communicate the inflection and pace of her voice. Now she says, 'Punctuation sounds good. I mean, it doesn't have a sound like a letter has a sound, but it makes all the letters sound better. If writing had no punctuation, it would sound dull.'

Tracey adds, 'Punctuation can show your feelings. You can show feelings with punctuation, or with words, or with both.' Tracey uses exclamation marks to show happiness and excitement. She learned them from her classmate, Peter. Exclamation marks travelled like wildfire throughout Hoban's class. One child brought them in, and soon most of the children were using them. At last they had a substitute for the tall heavy letters they had used as first graders to show important words.

These are some of the children's explanations for exclamation marks:

Wendy: Use them when you want it expressed out. They tell you were surprised.

Shawn: It makes a louder sound. It's like a demand, an order.

Diane: It changes the way people read the words. They read them faster. It's like an action word. Run! Quick!

Exclamations also spread quickly throughout the first grade at Atkinson. One six-year-old says, 'They mean you are happy, like it's your birthday.' Other first graders called them a 'surprise mark,' and 'excited mark.' Six year old Sharon confessed, 'I don't use them much because my books aren't exciting'.

Quotation marks, like exclamations, are popular with writers. They, too, give voice to print. Even first graders want their characters to talk like real people. One six-year-old put comic strip balloons around spoken sections in her stories until her teacher taught her the conventional way to show quotations.

A curriculum guide does not tell Ms Gerry when her first graders are ready for punctuation. Instead she follows the children. 'When their characters begin to talk, I show the children quotation marks', she says.

Third grade writers use quotations easily. 'You use quotations to tell it in a different voice,' Wendy says. 'And quotations make it shorter. Usually if you want to tell something is being said, it is quickest and shortest to just put it into quotes.'

More than half of Ms Hoban's class used the sound of their writing to explain periods. Chip says, 'As you read along in what you've written, you listen to your voice and when it gets lower, that's where you put the period in.'

Forty-seven percent of the explanations *writers* gave for punctuation referred to the way it affects the pace and inflection of language. Only nine percent of the *non-writers'* definitions referred to this.

Writers Go Beyond Titles

When children write, they care less about the official rules and names for punctuation than about how they are used. When six-year-old Jennice used quote marks, a researcher asked her, 'What's that?'

'Um, ah, oh, that thing, you know . . .' was her response.

'Well, when do you use them?' she was asked.

Jennice had a ready answer. 'When they talk,' she said. 'You know, when they say things.'

The non-writers rarely gave operational definitions. Instead, they described punctuation by trying to remember the rules they'd been taught. Ms West's class knew periods come at the end of a sentence. But when the researcher asked them where to end a sentence, they didn't know. 'You can tell where to end it by the period,' was all they could say. One boy had mastered the tricks of the trade. He suggested you look and see if a capital letter comes next, and if so, insert the period. The boy will do well on the third grade achievement tests. Probably many of his classmates will, as well. But drills on missing punctuation have little carry-over into writing.

Jack learned commas are for lists of people—Joe, Frank, Peter. 'Anywhere else?' the researcher asked. 'Sometimes when you paint,' Jack said. 'Different colors—purple, green, blue.' Then he added, 'But nowhere else'. Many of the 'mechanics' students defined commas by referring to one specific use only. 'Put it in between fruit.' 'Commas separate states.'

The writers didn't refer to rules but to their writing. Amy explains commas this way:

> If you have a long sentence and you want to keep it all there, you put a comma in to take a breath. If you were to make a new sentence, you'd change it up. One example is my flying piece of writing, I said, 'We got a little lower and over the beach, I saw tiny coloured dots.'

Before and after the commas, they are both parts of the same sentence. Like the first half of the sentence is one paragraph, and the other half is the second paragraph . . . like two edges of the same idea.

Amy has learned punctuation in context. She has learned more than rules. She is developing an intuitive sense for the nuances of punctuation.

Why Writers Need Punctuation: They Write Well

In September, Beth Hoban's students only needed an average of 2.22 different kinds of punctuation to correctly punctuate a piece of writing, and they used an average of 1.25 different kinds. They wrote mostly simple sentences, without dialogue, sound effects, supportive information, or exclamations.

Since then, the children have learned to make their writing more colourful, more varied. They include special effects in their writing. 'I keep putting in new kinds of punctuation,' eight-year-old Andrea says, 'because I need them. Like sound effects—it takes weird punctuation to put *thud-thud* or *splat!* onto my paper.'

Steven tried several kinds of punctuation to accompany the ring of his alarm clock. First he wrote *Rrrr!* He erased it. 'That sounds too sudden, like it ends too quickly,' he explained. Steven's final draft reads, 'Rrrr . . . the alarm blasted on and on in my room.' Since then Steven has used three dots several times. 'To me it means one, two, three minutes went by.'

By February, Ms Hoban's children needed an average of 5.62 different kinds of punctuation in order for their writing to be correctly punctuated, and they used an average of five different kinds in one piece.

Why Writers Punctuate: They Revise

Ms Hoban's children use carets, asterisks, and dashes to move words about on the page. Like professional writers, they use their drafts as working manuscripts. They put words on the paper in order to get their hands on them.

When nine-year-old Susie finishes her two page story about finding a skunk in the garbage can, she says, 'Now I'll fix it up—take out some parts and add.' For a few minutes, she rereads her draft. 'I think I'll fix the whole story up,' she says, 'not just parts'. This time when Susie rereads, she circles sections which especially need work. She circles this section, her beginning:

Last night I accompanied my sister to empty the garbage. She started emptying the garbage while I was playing on the lawn. All of a sudden she shrieked, 'skunk'. My sister ran by. I started running too.

Susie retraces the pencil circle. 'On my next draft, I'll really fix that up,' she says. 'I'll put in more detail.' This is Susie's next draft:

The sky was full of stars, so I decided to join my sister while she emptied the garbage. When I got out on the grass I started playing around. I was doing cartwheels and summersaults. I heard a shriek.

'Skunk!' Jill yelled. All of a sudden the night seemed very scary. The dark shadows of big trees crept onto the yard. I did not want to be out there with a skunk.

This time, Susie rereads with pencil in hand. Each word is reconsidered, rechosen. 'After I do the big stuff, I do each word,' Susie explains. With a caret, she inserts her sister's name into the first sentence. She reads it out loud.

... I decided to join my sister, Jill, while she emptied the garbage.

'Now I can just use her name, later on.' Susie says. She reads the next line out loud.

... When I got on the grass I started playing around. I was doing cartwheels and summersaults.

Her pencil paused over the phrase, 'I started playing around'. 'Do I need this?' she whispered to herself. The phrase was slashed, two sentences became one, and a comma was added. Now Susie adds a paragraph sign before 'All of a sudden the night seemed . . .'

'I have to work a long, long time on a little section if I want it to be perfect.' She says. Susie needs punctuation in order to consolidate and expand her sentences, to adjust her words, and to change her sequences. She uses asterisks, colons, carets, parentheses—punctuation marks that are often not taught until the middle school years.

These lists show the number of children from each of the two third grades who correctly described each type of punctuation:

Writing Class (total = 18)		*Mechanics Class (total = 16)*	
period	18	period	13
exclamation mark	16	exclamation mark	8
question mark	16	question mark	10
apostrophe	14	apostrophe	4
paragraph sign	13	paragraph sign	0
dash	12	dash	4
caret	11	caret	0
quotation marks	11	quotation marks	2
comma	10	comma	3
colon	8	colon	0
parentheses	7	parentheses	0
asterisk	7	asterisk	0
semicolon	1	semicolon	0

Children from both classes prefer exclamation marks, dashes, and apostrophes to commas. Teachers think commas are a simple, basic kind of punctuation but writers and non-writers, both, find them elusive.

The order of the two lists is similar. But writers know many more types of punctuation.

How Writers Learn Punctuation

When children need punctuation in order to be seen and heard, they become vacuum cleaners, sucking up odd bits from books, their classmates' papers, billboards and magazines. They find punctuation everywhere, and make it their own.

Six-year-old Casey doesn't know his consonant blends or all of his vowel sounds yet, but he uses exclamation marks. He brings his paper to his teacher.

THE BAD GI! FOS FVD WS TO SONK!

They read, 'the bad guys' force field was too strong'. Ms Gerry is surprised. 'Where did you learn these?' she asks, pointing to the exclamation marks.

Casey isn't sure. He thinks he found them on a friend's paper. 'It makes it sound more scarier,' he says. 'You put them after a word, any word.'

Even if writers have never used a mark of punctuation, they are usually familiar with it. Shawn recognised the colon. 'My Dad uses them in his writing,' he says. 'But one thing; I can't read his writing.'

Melissa nods at the sight of the ellipsis. 'Those three periods; people use them at the end of paragraphs. But I usually just use one period.'

Across the hall, the mechanics students were baffled and amazed at many of the punctuation marks. 'Are those English?' they asked. 'I've never seen half of them.' They hadn't seen them because they had no use for them.

When children need punctuation they not only see it, they remember what they see. On April 9th, first grader Chris, used a comma in a series. He wrote:

I went through prickers, over boulders and other junk.

Later the researcher asked Chris's teacher when she had taught him the comma. 'I didn't,' she said and then looked back over her records to be sure. She found that on the 17th of January, Chris had been working at the conference table while she showed two other children how to use commas. Now, three months later, the seven-year-old had used what he learned through eavesdropping.

When Ms Gerry reads Chris's story, she will respond first to the content. She will listen to Chris's description of the trail, and ask what 'other junk' refers to. Only later does she look at punctuation.

She admires Chris's commas, and helps him with quotations. They find missing periods and question marks, so she sends him off to reread his paper and correct it. 'You've got a terrific story here,' she says. 'It's worth working on.'

Writer becomes editor. Chris reads his words out loud, listening to his voice. Line by line, word by word, he scrutinises his page. 'Real writers have a boss who tells them what to do and where to put punctuation,' the young writer says. 'But I have to do it myself.'

But Chris is glad to go over his page, making it perfect. He knows what he has to say is important. And punctuation is part of what he has to tell.

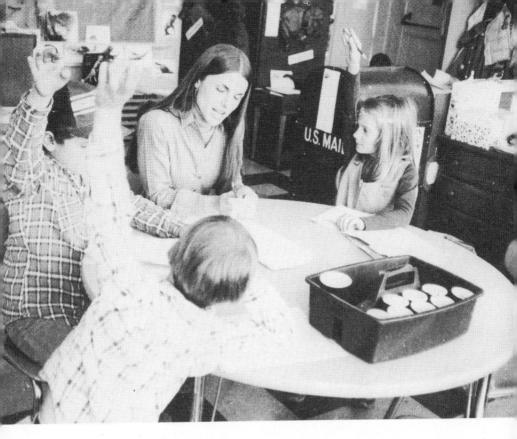

9. Making Time For Writing
Judith E. Egan

'HOW CAN I POSSIBLY FIT MORE WRITING into a day which is already too short?' This was the question I found myself asking as I approached September and my second grade class. I had always provided a writing area in my activity-centred classroom but this year I wanted to offer more—I wanted to reorganise my daily schedule and focus more attention on the writing process, making it a priority in my Language Arts program. Time was the major factor until I decided to dedicate the mornings to the teaching of writing and allow that to become the basis from which all other Language Arts concepts would emerge. This meant letting go of many traditional and 'safe' methods and materials which I had used for years. Having made such a commitment, however, caused me to search for more effective methods.

The morning in our classroom now consists of three sections. As the day begins, children are working in activity areas including those working on current pieces of writing. Another group is preparing for a writing conference to be held later in the morning. During this time, I work with a small group on a skill area needing introduction or reinforcement, as has been evidenced by the children's reading and writing efforts. The second part of the morning allows me the time to circulate among the various activities, helping in any way I can. The third finds me working in individual writing conferences. At this time, the child reads his finished piece to me and we discuss any skills needing attention, focusing on one or two at most. During this final period, I might also meet with a few children in a group conference where writer critiques writer.

Time for writing is no longer a concern of mine. The re-organisation of my schedule and the realisation that writing is not an isolated subject has allowed me to have a much stronger sense of accomplishment and individualised instruction. I realise now I didn't need to *make* time for writing as it goes on constantly throughout each day. Children not only write in the Writing area but choose to write about Science, Block, Listening and Math activities. In our Pretend area, the children write lengthy scripts for plays and puppet shows which are later viewed and critiqued by the class. Before, my Language Arts time emphasised reading. Now I find that I can emphasise writing and even exceed the reading standards I used to maintain. When children write, they read and more importantly become critical readers since they are authors themselves. To my second graders, the satisfaction received from writing is well worth the effort involved.

10. Who Says That Children Can't Write the First Week of School?

Mary Ellen Giacobbe

CHILDREN SAY THEY CAN WRITE but that they can not read. They can hold a crayon, marker, pencil or some other kind of writing instrument and they can produce some form of written expression.

When this school year began I wanted to find out what my first graders attending the Atkinson Academy, the public school in Atkinson, New Hampshire, could do as writers. On the first day of school I gave five of them a nine inch by twelve inch journal containing forty sheets of unlined paper. I told them that the journals were for them to write in. The other seventeen children were assigned to other areas in the classroom.

I circulated around the classroom observing and talking with the children. "Tell me about your building.' ... 'Why do you think the sand goes through this strainer faster than through that strainer?' ... 'How many cubes do you think it will take to fit across the top of the desk?'

Someone tugged at my sleeve and I turned to see Mark standing by my side with his journal. 'Tell me about your drawing, Mark,' I said.

He pointed to each part of the drawing and said, 'This is the ocean and this is a sailboat and this is the anchor. These are clouds.'

He had written BD for boat and KLD for cloud. I could tell that the oversized anchor was important but he felt that he couldn't write anchor, so I helped him.

'Can I do another page?' he asked.

I nodded and Mark rejoined Ellen at the writing table. Ellen was tracing her hand with a blue marker. With a red marker she coloured the entire centre and thumb and then continued to colour the fingers orange, purple, brown and black. A big yellow sun appeared in the top right corner and two flowers grew to the left of the hand. Short, straight, vertical, green lines bordered the bottom of the page. Ellen wrote:

THE TRCE WAS TACAN A WEC

(The turkey was taking a walk.)

She read it to herself, crossed out the *T* in *Tacan,* changed it to a *w* and on top of *a wec,* she wrote *D the hall.* Her message now read:

THE TRCE WAS WACAN D THE HALL

(The turkey was walking down the hill.)

Already Ellen knew that she could change her message so that it said exactly what she wanted it to say. She was rereading and revising.

My attention was drawn to the tap, tap, tapping of the black marker on David's page as he was creating a snowstorm. He wrote:

I SO SO

(I saw snow.)

David said, 'This is a big snowstorm. A real blizzard.' As he touched each word, he read, 'I saw snow.'

I asked David, 'What do you notice about the words *saw* and *snow?*' He replied, 'They both begin with the same sound.'

Lisa's marker was filling the page with one inch letters to tell about her drawing of a huge blue circle with a yellow and a white dot in the centre. I joined her on the rug just as she was finishing:

TES IS A PEKHTR

(This is a picture.)

'Could you tell me more about your picture, Lisa?' I asked.

She turned the page and replied, 'In just a minute.' As she continued to write, a duck and a pond became obvious. Her message:

AV A POND AND A DAK

(of a pond and a duck)

Throughout the morning the children who weren't writing were asking, 'When am I going to get my book?' . . . 'Can I have a book like those guys? . . . 'Am I going to get my book tomorrow?'

By the third day of school all twenty-two children had their own journals and were all writing. I knew that children could write sooner than we think but I thought it would take longer than three half-days of school before an entire class of five, six and seven year olds would be writers.

As the blank pages in their journals came alive with drawings and words telling of their experiences, I could see these children had entered school ready to engage in the active process of writing. They were writing their own workbooks. They were showing me what they knew as well as what they needed to know. There were no errors to be red pencilled. Just information showing me what the next step of instruction should be.

In my education courses, I had been taught that children must first be able to read and when they had a reading vocabulary they could begin to write. These children were contradicting that teaching. They could write even though they could not read. (However, they were usually able to read what they wrote!)

During the second week of school I administered a self-made writing test of twenty words. In choosing the words I tried to use as many different initial and final consonants and long and short vowels as possible. Fifteen of the words were one syllable and five were two syllable words.

I worked with the children individually or in pairs. I gave each a piece of paper eight and one-half by eleven and one-half inches, sectioned into rectangles numbered one through twenty. I asked the children to write the word *rag* next to the number one. I did not emphasise any sounds. I said the word as I would in normal conversation. I continued with the rest of the test in the same manner.

After ninety minutes of testing, I learned that my first grade children were able to write far more than I ever imagined. I wondered why I had waited so long to let my children write in other years. Figure 1 shows the results from a sampling of the test. Four of the words used in the test are written across the top. The childrens' responses are listed below. Jeremy and Ed had come to school able to write most words accurately. Helen was able to write the initial sounds of words.

Figure 1—Class Spelling Patterns—First Week of School

	rag	five	buzz	doctor
Ellen	rag	fiv	Bozo	Dokr
Helen	ro	FS	B	D
Frank	F	F	P	D
Greg	Rag	Fly	Bis	Dldi
John	RAKG	FAF	8AS	DAODR
Brian	rɔg	Ɉif	das	dodr
Jennifer	RAG	FIve	BIS	DOCTR
Lisa	RAG	FOYV	BAS	DOCTR
Kelly	RIG	FIV	BIS	DIR

Bob	RAG	FA	BSS	DIr
Carl	RaG	FiFv	Bis	DOKR
Linda	RAG	viN	BST	DKT
Sarah	RAG	FIV	BIZ	DOR
Diane	Rag	fuv	buz	Dorsc
Donna	rag	foif	Bus	Doud
David	Rag	Fiv	Baz	DOCtr
Jeremy	RAG	FiVE	Buzz	DOCTER
Ed	RAG	FiVE	Buzz	DOCTOR
Mark	iA	FF	BS	DT
Susan	raG	Fiv	BU	DOD

The responses of four children are shown for the entire test of twenty words in Figure 2.

Jennifer and Lisa knew all of the consonant sounds and were able to use them when writing a word. They were also using vowels. Bob was writing most initial and final consonants with a sprinkling of vowels. Mark was writing *r* in the medial position in *zero* but did not hear *r* in the initial position in *rag,* or at the end of *doctor.*

What I Found Out

1. Most of the children felt this was an activity they could do.
2. Only two said, 'I don't know how to write.'
3. The two children who said they did not know how to write did not know all of their letters. Ken would say, 'Buzz. Buh, buh. B. What does a B look like?' He was hearing the sound; he could reproduce the sound and give it a letter name but he could not remember what the letter looked like.
4. Some children said, 'Is that right?' I would reply, 'What do you think?' They would respond, 'It sounds that way to me!' or 'That's all I hear.'
5. All of the children wrote in a left to right direction.
6. Most of the children knew the initial and final consonant sounds and were able to use them in writing a word.

The children did not stop writing at the end of the first week of school. They have been writing continuously for almost three months. Their words now make sentences and their sentences tell stories. Forty-seven books have been typed and sewn into hard covers which have become their reading. Because my children write, they now say, 'Yes, we can read!'

Figure 2—Spelling Patterns—Twenty Words—First Week of School

	rag	buzz	lid	six	game	nice	doctor	view	yellow	kiss
Jennifer	RAG	BIS	LeD	sics	GAM	NIS	DOCTR	VUW	YeLLD	KISS
Lisa	RAG	BAS	LED	SECS	GAM	NAIYS	DOCTR	VYU	YLO	KES
Bob	RAG	BSS	LD	S	GMA	N	DIr	VU		CS
Mark	iA	BS	LED	SS	KM	NS	DT	UO	LO	KiSS

	camp	zero	hill	tack	five	pickle	muffin	wife	job	quick
Jennifer	KAP	ZARO	HAL	TAK	FIVe	PICL	MIFN	WIF	JOB	CWC
Lisa	KEP	SERO	HEL	TAC	FOYV	PECL	MFEN	WAIYF	GOB	COEC
Bob	CAP	SiO	HLLL	TAC	FA	PCL	MAF	WAF	LOP	CWC
Mark	KP	SRO	UL	TK	FF	PL	MFA	WAF	GB	KWK

11. Revision in the Writer's Workshop and in the Classroom

Donald M. Murray and *Donald H. Graves*

IN AN ATTEMPT TO EXPLORE THE REVISION PROCESS *The Journal of Education* invited a writer, who is also a researcher into the writing process, to keep a journal while he was revising a novel and several pieces of non-fiction. We also invited a researcher into the writing process, who is also a writer, to comment on the writer's journal and to point out the classroom implications of the writer's testimony.

The writer is Donald M. Murray, a Professor of English at the University of New Hampshire, who won the Pulitzer Prize for Journalism and who has published poetry, short stories, non-fiction juveniles, novels, magazine articles, a textbook for teachers, *A Writer Teaches Writing,* a composition program for elementary schools, and many journal articles on the writing process.

During the period when he kept this journal—September 19, 1979 to December 8, 1979—he revised a novel of more than 300 manuscript pages and revised four pieces of non-fiction.

Donald H. Graves, the researcher, a Professor of Education at the University of New Hampshire, is Director of the Writing Process Laboratory, research editor of *Language Arts,* and has just completed a study for the Ford Foundation on the status of writing, *Balance the Basics: Let Them Write.*

Graves is now working full time on an NIE funded study of the writing processes of six, seven, eight, and nine year old children. Through the direct observation of children with video and hand recordings, he and his two research associates, Susan Sowers and Lucy Calkins, are completing the second year of daily observation of sixteen children as they write, as well as large group data from children in nine different classrooms in the same two year period.

MURRAY	GRAVES

☐ Yesterday, Aviva called and, apologetically, asked me to cut my chapter on 'The Feel of Writing' from sixteen pages to twelve. She was surprised at my delight. Given no choice but to cut, I become the surgeon. It would go fast, and I knew the piece would be better for the surgery.

☐ Steph pointed out in my draft of a chapter for the Donovan-McClelland book that I incorrectly used 'for' in the second paragraph. She suggested 'because'. My reaction was normal; I rejected her suggestion, as I would any editor's suggestion. I over-reacted and rewrote the whole paragraph. When I receive criticism, I normally put the draft aside and start a new one. It is probably the way I reestablish control over my territory. Childish. But the paragraph was better. 'For' became 'who'.

Rebellion is not the exclusive property of the professional writer. I find it a healthy sign when children rebel in order to maintain control of their information or language. The child may be 'wrong', but the greater issue in the long run will be the child's sense of control of the writing process. We are experts at stealing children's writing voices.

☐ The principal changes in the chapter for Donovan and McClelland were inserts which developed important points towards the end of the piece or which wove concepts from the early part of the piece through the rest of it. The early pages were rewritten many, many times. The changes were reinforcements of what was discovered through the early rewriting of the beginning.

Our data show that children as young as eight years of age are capable of writing to *find out* what they mean. For such children, six to ten unassigned drafts is not unusual.

☐ Yesterday I drafted a tentative new beginning of the novel; revising becoming rehearsing. I know what

Murray has a different pace than that permitted in most school situations. He waits, listens, has to happen in the new beginning. In addition to all the usual things, such as introducing the story, the main characters, setting the scene, establishing the voice, I have to allow Ian to discover the murder of Lucinda's children, which he didn't know in the last draft until the middle of the novel. Sometime this summer, I realised he had to know from the beginning and that knowledge would give a necessary energy to the beginning of the novel. I recalled William Gibson's advice in *Shakespeare's Game*, 'A play begins when a world in some state of equipoise, always uneasy, is broken by a happening.'

suspends judgment. He is surprised by his characters and information. The waiting is the best aid to redrafting. 'Oh, this is missing. I forgot to say why he was upset.' Papers due within the same class period, or even in the short space of a few days, do not aid listening or that important sense of ownership of the writing.

☐ I don't think while writing; I see. I watched him find the old newspaper clippings, saw, felt his reaction to the news. I do not think what Ian should do; I watch him and record what he does. And yet the technical problem has been thought out before. Planted. Was the scene I watched what grew from that seed?

To cut sixteen pages to twelve for Aviva, I count the lines on a page—twenty-seven—estimate where editorial changes have added lines, and come up with a total: one hundred nine lines to cut.

I have observed surgeons. I cut fast, clean strokes, no hesitation, and subtract each line from the total. Thirty minutes, and I am at the end and have cut one hundred seventeen lines, eight over. I cut eight hundred twenty-seven words and added sixty-seven. I have eight lines to use to clarify, restore, or develop if necessary. Now I go through and look at the notes in the margins of copies I have given colleagues, after I have cut on instinct.

Starting with first grade, children have to become proficient in the time-space dimensions of writing on paper. 'This will be a two page paper; oh, I'm stuck, where will I put this long word?'

☐ As I walked home from school today I rehearsed yesterday's idea. I could start the novel without a new first chapter, weaving the new material through the old.

When children write regularly, they rehearse while watching TV, riding on buses, in all sorts of places. Just knowing they will write every day enables them to think about writing when they are not actually writing. Professional writers 'panic' at the thought of losing one day's writing, simply because it ruins thinking in between writing sessions. Picking up the cold trail for amateur or pro is a disheartening task. Children who compose as few as two to three times a week, lose out on the important thinking that goes on between writing episodes.

□ Revision of one article I am doing is not revision by my definition. There are no new visions or insights, just simple editing for clarification. It is a bad article. It needs no work, has no possibilities hidden between its words.

□ When I reread a draft and disgust cramps my bowels, I've learned to back off. It's taken me a long time to realise that I can't force a solution to a writing problem. What do I do when I'm stuck? I quit.

□ It has taken me years to realise that quitting doesn't make you a quitter. The football coach still yells in my ear. I keep coming back to the writing desk and keep quitting— without guilt (without too much guilt).

The 'can I have another piece of paper' syndrome is in many class-rooms, especially where there are good readers who write infrequently. Their writing tools lag well behind their ability to read. They are painfully aware of the discrepancy between their written text and what they wish they could say.

□ I am surprised how calm I am at the slow start of the revision of the novel. I feel it is perking, somewhere. I have identified a technical problem in the first chapter—the dialogue on the telephone—and I have a rough sequence of action. I have to get to the typewriter and that's not easy with the teaching schedule I've established for myself. I resent this dependence on the typewriter to get this revision going. Usually I revise by pen, but this particular Olympia Electric is necessary on these pages in some way I can't understand. Perhaps I have to make the writing real by seeing it in type. That may make it an object that I can study.

Children erase, make brushing movements as if to make the paper crisp and clean. Sometimes they need to recopy, just to see it lined up, or just to simulate what final copy might be like. Unfortunately, too many children are intolerant of cross-outs and manipulations needed to make the text 'messy in order to make it clear' (Calkins 1979).

☐ Beginnings are terrifying. You have to capture the reader instantly, and there is so much exposition and description that has to be wound into the narrative, so it can rapidly uncoil in the reader's mind.

Six year olds are not terrified in the least. But with each passing year, as a sense of options, or fear of failure, or growing sense of audience appears, the terror of the blank page becomes more real. This fear occurs with the best of teaching. Imagine the terror of the blank page when the teacher is punitive!

☐ I have to make sure that the new beginning is in the voice of the novel. Each piece of work has its own voice. If that voice is strong and I can hear it then I can easily return and confidently revise after interruptions. If the voice isn't clear, then I don't have a piece of writing, and there's no point in revising.

☐ I rarely refer to the notes I make about a work in process during the writing.

☐ I have been working on the novel in my head but I am being drawn into the drafting by a force like gravity.

☐ Chapter one just took off, and I'm running after it as fast as I can.

☐ I was outside the novel and then, by writing, I was inside it. I have no longer any conscious consideration of technical matters. The novel has begun to tell me what to do.

☐ I waited patiently, and now the story is working. I have three pages of draft without consciously selecting from the dozens of strategic choices in my journal and in my head.

Three pages in thirty-five minutes. I'm itching to start the next novel. The better one piece of writing is going, the more insistently the other pieces demand writing. There is an explosion of possibility. I want to do poems, stories, articles, plays—to prune, to paint.

When children receive more time for writing, and on a regular basis, they learn to wait more effectively. When children wait, they may conference with the teacher, or with other children, or just sit and read what they have already written. This gives distance to the text and greatly aids the act of revision.

And waiting is the prelude to the creative burst. It is rare, whether the writer be child or professional, that the *high quality burst* is not preceded by effective listening and waiting. Such activity has great carry-over to other curricular areas, simply because the child is in touch with himself or herself as a learner. Listening does that.

As educators, I think we have to ask ourselves if we provide such high quality listening time for children with our over-inflated curricula and time slots that must be filled.

Regular writing helps children to put the spelling and mechanical aspects of writing behind them. Only then can children give greater attention to the information. Regular daily writing with effective challenge and response to the writing, aids the writer to reflect on the craft itself.

☐ I am aware, when I am writing as fast as I was this morning, that I am weaving threads, but I am not conscious of picking up the threads and using them any more than an experienced weaver is conscious of the learned act of weaving. I simply sense the need for action, referring back to a previous action, for setting up the beginning of a new pattern, of drawing together, knotting, loosening up, busy, busy, busy, at my clattering loom, but not thinking. Doing. That's the best thing about craft, you can get beyond thinking.

☐ Is it the vocation of the artist to celebrate life by showing the moments of order within disorder? The greater the art, the more temporary these orders? Or the more the artist makes us aware of the forces threatening the temporary order, the more moving the work?

☐ It is one of those rare mornings when the desk is clear, my tools are at hand, Mozart is on the radio, and the autumn sun pours through the yellow, baring trees. I feel happy —and I have a slight headache, a bit of cramp in the bowels, fear that the work will not go—or go well. But the timer is on. I must type up what is written to get to the point where I can weld the new beginning to the previous draft.

☐ The draft is rolling. It is developing, increasing, growing full with additional information, revelations, connections. I follow it as it speaks, and then when it is really going well, I am compelled to step back, to go to the john, heat another cup of coffee, put a record on the phonograph, stand back, get distance, see if it is really going as well as I thought.

☐ I am happiest when making imaginary worlds; I am still the only child whose playmates live in the walls.

☐ This writing must be like skiing Tuckerman, hurtling down, almost out of control, the skis not quite touching the snow, faster, faster.

☐ If I type my own draft a hundred times, I would write a hundred different novels, for this imagined world is so real and has so many dimensions it can be seen a hundred different ways.

☐ Fitting, joining, cutting, shaping, smoothing—the busy cabinetmaker in his shop.

☐ Is there enough? Too much? Again and again, line by line, paragraph by paragraph, page by page, I must ask these same questions. And answering them by writing, ask them again of the new lines.

☐ It is easy to move chunks of writing around, or to fit new chunks in. There is never one way, but many ways.

Murray mentions that he is *compelled* to step back from his writing. During the high point of an episode, I have seen children get up to sharpen pencils, wander around the room (where permitted) or talk to another child. This is particularly true if the child is trying something new, a logical transition not tried before, or a new description. The intensity of engagement actually demands disengagement.

'How long should it be? Are there pages enough?' The concept, 'It is good if it is long,' begins at age six and continues on through advanced doctoral degrees. Small wonder that the idea of cutting rarely enters into the teaching of writing. Through effective questions, teachers can elicit information needed to heighten one section and thereby make other sections seem unnecessary. Such questions as, 'Tell me in one sentence what this is about,' can be a help with cutting.

The use of carets, wide margins, scissors and paste, for reorganising an early draft is useful for young writers. With daily writing and good teacher conferences, there is a cluster of eight-year-olds who are ready for this kind of activity. Too many children see writing, particularly their own, as fixed, immovable. They need to see how it can be moved around and with profit. If teachers model these tools of reorganisation with their own writing, children can see how the space-time issues of writing are solved in revision. We can live a lifetime and never see craftspersons revising their work.

☐ Reading your own prose is an act of faith. It takes courage to leave in, not to cut, not to change.

☐ I am suspicious when it works the way I want it to work.

☐ Writing without thought. Just writing. Not thinking about writing and then writing, but writing/ thinking, writing that is thought.

☐ There comes a time when you have to admit that the work can't be perfect. It will never match the vision.

Teachers who sense that an impossible road of perfection is defeating a writer, need to help the writer to end the selection. They can even model an ending to their own writing. 'It isn't perfect. I *feel* it isn't where I want it to be, but I am going to end the piece just the same.' Children *need to see their teachers write,* not to copy but to sense their involvement in the task of writing.

☐ Put something in on one side of the draft and something pops out on the other.

☐ (From a letter I wrote to another writer . . .) 'I've gotten the first draft of the first chapter of the novel revised and typed and moved ahead to those dreadful, awful, terrible chapters immediately after the first chapter (the first third of the novel.) I knew that they would read like shit, but I knew that if I could grit my teeth I could face them and fight my way through. I sailed through them in a matter of hours, and I saw that the piece of writing had demanded the new beginning I thought so radical. To put it

When the beginning is right the rest follows, and more quickly. As young writers develop, they learn to make decisions about the content of their writing at an earlier time. For example, some children do effective decision-making at the point of topic choice. One topic is chosen, two excluded. Indeed, this can be an effective movement of revision. Then there are those who will try three to five leads. The more advanced the writer, the more they realise the importance of early decisions.

differently, I thought I would have to make a lot of changes to justify the new beginning. In fact, the "changes" were made before the new beginning.'

☐ It took me from spring to autumn to create the new beginning of the novel. To put it differently, it took me months to hear what the novel had to tell me about its story. If I had listened to the draft it would have told me how to begin the novel. It did tell me. When I found the right beginning there were no major changes to be made in the text. The novel was waiting to be begun that way.

☐ I am completely within the text. I start to add a sentence, and it is already there, written last January, just the way I would write it now. It must be the right sentence.

☐ I wonder if extensive rewriting is not mostly a failure of prewriting, or allowing adequate time for rehearsal, a matter of plucking the fruit before it is ripe.

☐ But you have to bite the fruit to know it is really ripe.

☐ Much of the reordering in the text is making sure that the most important material is at the point of emphasis in the paragraph, in the sentence, in the scene. Where are the points of emphasis? At the end and at the beginning. The important information must be those points.

This is the same location of attention with the young writers —beginnings and endings. For the young writers this is the easiest location to help them with revision.

☐ It's so hard to go back and face your copy. It is a mirror. It does not show the person you hoped to be but the person you are.

☐ This page explodes with possibility. I must control it. I see a thousand stories at once, each superimposed on the other.

Children who find that their selection is about two or three subjects, not one, should not be dismayed. When they keep a list of future topics, or collections of discarded material cut out of other drafts, they already have a start on another selection. No extra writing is ever wasted. They are merely shards of rehearsal for another selection.

☐ I hear myself say in my head what I read on the page seconds later.

☐ The biggest problem in revising this morning is my itchy nose. I must be allergic to my own prose.

☐ I have to keep stepping back, read a few pages of something else, keep my distance, or I'll be drawn into the story.

Students need help with the process of gaining distance. Teachers help through the writing conference. 'What did you have in mind here? Underline the one line that says more than any other what this selection is about.'

☐ Sometimes I am drawn into my story. This is the reality, and I look back at the writer, at the desk, wondering who he is, why is he bent over, his nose almost touching his knuckles, making marks on paper, muttering to himself.

Stand back and watch an entire group of children in the process of writing. Some compose with their noses *on* the paper; others put their cheeks on the paper and look across at their pens writing; others squirm and jump in their chairs, place knees on the desk, whereas others lean far back, almost to the point of retreat.

☐ The story makes jagged unexpected moves. I laugh in surprise and chase after it.

☐ After revising, I am much more observant when I walk to school, noticing the way women stalk in boots, how the three North African students gesture to each other. I see a man turn from a woman and I make up reasons, whole movies in my mind.

☐ In revision, we are constantly adjusting distance, the distance between writer and experience, writer and meaning, writer and the writing, writer and reader, language and subject, text and reader.

☐ I have only one reader while I am revising—myself. I am trying to make this page come clear. That's all.

Children do extensive reading when they reread and revise their own texts. Just how much reading is involved in the writing process is just beginning to dawn on our research team. Large amounts of time have been taken from formal reading instruction and given over to time for writing in rooms where the study is being conducted. Surprisingly, reading scores did not go down; they went up... and significantly. Since writing is the *making of reading,* children may decode for ideas differently than if they had never written at all.

☐ The writer has a split brain—creator and critic—or competing forces—freedom and discipline.

☐ There is no right or wrong, just what works within this situation.

Or, as one teacher in Scotland told me, 'I don't speak of the paper as right or wrong. It is only finished or unfinished. That's the way it is with art.'

☐ Every change in the text affects the text fore and aft, sets off a chain reaction of new meanings.

At about the age of eight, with effective conferences, there is a growing group of advanced writers who recognise the effect that one change can have on an entire selection. Recognising the relationship of parts and wholes is an important developmental phenomena.

☐ The mad weaver keeps dozens of threads in his mind, weaving so hard he is only rarely aware of the weaving, and worried when he becomes aware of it. His weaving should appear natural, not contrived. He contrives to be natural.

☐ How do you know what works? By the satisfying sound it makes when it clicks into place.

☐ Why is it so hard to get working when it is so good to be lost within the experience, to lose all sense of time until there is a sudden coming to, and I stretch. My legs, arms, back, are stiff, as if I had been asleep or in a trance.

☐ I think I have made no changes within a page, but I count two hundred thirteen words put in and taken out.

☐ What do I do when I revise? I read to add what is needed to be there, cut

Without knowing it, Murray has just listed the developmental order what isn't needed, reorder what must be moved.

☐ I hear my writing as loud as if I speak it. Sometimes I do speak it. The final test is always, 'How does it sound?'

☐ Yesterday I read some of the novel in Becky's class. It is helpful to read before an audience. I heard Frank's voice in my voice, clearer than I had ever heard it when I wrote it.

☐ Each day I learn to write. No, each day I learn to see. If I can see clearly the writing will be easy.

☐ Revision, or perhaps rehearsal for revision, goes on all the time—while I am in the car, walking to class, waiting for a meeting to start, eating, going to sleep, watching television. I constantly revise in my head, fitting things together to see if they work. I am convinced that what I know of this activity is only a small proportion of what goes on while I am awake and while I am asleep. My head is constantly writing.

☐ The satisfaction of rearranging words is a physical satisfaction. Once you have the order right, you can thump a sentence the way a trucker thumps tires. The sentence will give off a satisfying sound.

☐ The quality of the writing often comes from detail.

in which children learn to revise: (1) Add material, (2) Cut, (3) Reorder.

How does it sound? Does it sound exciting, beautiful, funny? Children strive to put the sounds of speech back into their writing through prosodic markers (darkened letters, capitals for points of emphasis), the use of exclamation points, over-use of interjections, or conversation. Children are bothered by the silence of their words on the page. They like 'noisy' pages.

Rehearsal is an important act for all writers. Children are no exception. Rehearsal begins with drawing (when children need to *see* what they mean) just prior to the act of writing. Gradually, children rehearse farther from the actual act of writing. Or, the first draft becomes a rehearsal for the second. Rehearsals become more frequent and tentative. Daily writing leads to an increase in effective rehearsal. The most difficult writing of all, is that writing where rehearsal begins simultaneously to the assignment. When children write infrequently, this is precisely what happens, and is one of the major reasons why writing is the hated act. Indeed, unfamiliarity breeds contempt.

☐ The piece of writing detaches itself from the writer. The writer can look at it as if it were a stranger—the daughter who comes to visit with a new husband. She—and the draft—is familiar and strange at the same time.

☐ I like to revise by hand so that I can enter into the text the way a surgeon plunges his hands down into a body and messes around.

☐ I hear the words as I use them. Revising is an act of talking to myself. I sound out the words, testing them by my ear, listening to how they sound in relation to each other.

☐ Revision requires a special kind of reading. The reader/writer must keep all strands of the past writing in mind, and yet maintain a vision of what *may* come, of what is coming clear through the writing.

This is the same person who changes one sentence, yet sees the effect on the whole. But this person has a different pace, is a student of listening to the text. The teacher provides for this stance through a much slower pace for written selections as well as listening-type questions in the writing conference. Teachers who provide a slower pace do not lower demands or expectations. Actually, it is a much higher level of demand because the student must learn to listen to his/her voice rather than that of the teacher.

☐ Writing is a puzzle with no one solution. There are always many right solutions. Any one you choose sets up new puzzles.

☐ There is no such thing as free writing. The work takes over and establishes its own discipline. The piece of writing has momentum, energy—a river in flood. Learning to be a writer is learning to go with the flood.

The work can take over when the teacher consciously works for students to find their own voices and to be responsive to the effect of voice on information. Students must teach teachers about their subjects, whether it be grade one or a dissertation.

☐ I knead language, pound it, stretch it, shape it, work it; I am up to my elbows in language.

☐ Reading what isn't—yet—on the page is a special skill only distantly related to reading what is printed on the page.

☐ Revising is, in part, a matter of making up reasons for what worked by accident, or at least what wasn't made consciously. It is the rational end of an irrational process. The intent often comes after the act.

The intent can come later if audience is not introduced too soon into the writing process. Too much store is put in knowing an audience before the writer begins. It may be that intent and audience are both discovered in the later stages of revision. To be responsive to oneself, my own voice, the information before me, demands the suspension of both intent and audience.

☐ The surprise during writing of reading what you have written. You thought you knew what you were going to write, you thought you knew what you were writing, now you find out what you have written.

Index